OZ RESIDENCE / STANLEY SAITOWITZ NATOMA ARCHITECTS

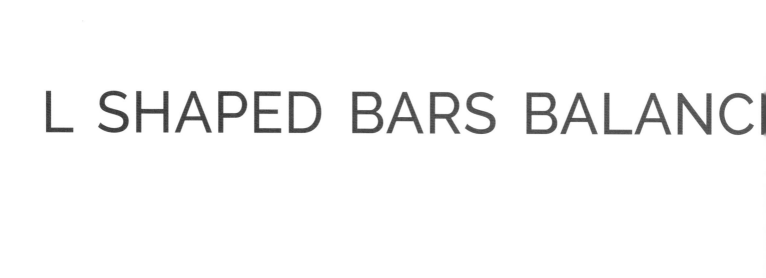

ON TOP OF EACH OTHER

MASTERPIECE
SERIES

OZ RESIDENCE / STANLEY SAITOWITZ NATOMA ARCHITECTS

FOREWORD BY DAVID WARNER | INTRODUCTION BY AARON BETSKY
EPILOGUE BY STANLEY SAITOWITZ | PHOTOGRAPHY BY RICHARD BARNES & BRUCE DAMONTE

OSCAR RIERA OJEDA
PUBLISHERS

CONTENTS

FOREWORD BY DAVID WARNER	010
INTRODUCTION BY AARON BETSKY	012
DESIGN	016
DESCRIPTION	018
PRESENTATION DRAWINGS	022
CONSTRUCTION	044
WORKING DRAWINGS	046
PROCESS	066
BUILDING	098
EPILOGUE BY STANLEY SAITOWITZ	168
APPENDIX	186
PROJECT CREDITS	188
PHOTOGRAPHY CAPTIONS	190
DESIGNERS	194
BUILDERS	196
BOOK CREDITS	200

FOREWORD
BY DAVID WARNER

When building iconic architecture, where standard systems are expressed through dynamic, cutting-edge craftsmanship, there comes a moment when an "all-hands-on-deck" approach is necessary.

All field construction team members work in concert with the various consultants, especially those working in the structural field, to form a single kinetic relationship. This complete group effort creates amazing structures with a range of components, not just those used to express large, dramatic shapes; loading sequences, cantilevers, openings, etc.

In the case of Oz, concrete was truly pushed to the limit both structurally, and as an aesthetic that would be exposed as part of the building's final look. To accomplish that took an incredible amount of effort, both in the forming that established the aesthetic parameters and the layout of the post-tensioning cables to create the cantilevers. The monolithic no cold-joint pouring needed to be sequenced in such a way as to allow homogenous large format installations throughout the day.

The most extreme aspect of the pour day was the fact that our project took up the entire capacity of all the concrete batch plants in the South Bay area, since servicing our project alone required the installation of over 400 yards of concrete for the ceiling and flooring decks of the house and its extremely pronounced cantilever formations.

To arrive at this point required months of forming, mechanical layouts, and future post-tensioning sequences, all of which were necessary to make sure that the crucially important pour day went off successfully. This included batch recipes that contained the necessary additives and reduced water to allow the concrete to chemically cure at a slow rate without the over-dehydration that would have caused imperfections.

There was no turning back once the concrete arrived at the job site and began to be placed inside the forms. There were over 100 personnel working on a single-family residence for that pour day, not including equipment operators, pumping systems, cranes, etc. We also had stand-by engineers testing samples for air entrainment and core samples for strength, all of which had to be coordinated as part of a huge effort. The operation began before dawn and ended after dusk and the results were amazing!

These are singularly successful moments in a building career, for both the contractor and the consultants landmarks in architectural heritage created thanks to Stanley Saitowitz's vision and design principles.

INTRODUCTION
BY AARON BETSKY

A House Without Noise
The Extreme Minimalism of Stanley Saitowitz

Conversation Between Stanley Saitowitz and Aaron Betsky, November 6, 2024

AB: The Oz House is quite a large one; it seems as if it is meant to be more than just a single-family home.

SS: Well, it serves that purpose, of course, but there's also a sense in which this is, as the name we gave it implies, Oz, up there on the top of the hill. The owners underwent a magical transformation from being college kids to being early members of a very large tech company in California. They have four kids, which means four bedroom suites and a principal, but the place is also meant for an extended family that is always around. That has led to a situation with, for instance, eight bedrooms. There's just always a lot of people there.

AB: But, compared to other such houses in or above Silicon Valley, this is a very stripped down building, not in terms of scale, or in technical ambition or even in volumetric complexity, but in terms of the way that it does not brag about itself or its view.

SS: Most people in the tech community do not have much connection to architecture, but these clients saw my work and wanted a modern building. But what I think what was so particular about this situation was that there was no real context for the house at all. Basically, it's a suburb, and there were no surrounding influences to work off. It was also a flat hilltop with a distant view. Quite honestly, the view was more abstract than perceived. My eyesight is good, and I could hardly see San Francisco when I was up there. You could see the Bay, but otherwise, there was almost nothing to work with, so the task was really to use the house to construct the place, and that's why there is this threading and weaving to make the site more dimensional and particular.

AB: And yet the natural impulse I would think would be to make a courtyard house with views out and sheltered spaces in between. When I look at the plans and the way the structure rises up and spirals around that captured space, which has not been landscaped to be an habitable space, it seems to be something different.

SS: That is more of an in-between space than a focal point. But, beyond the pool and up against the property line, there is a defined court which houses you, and then opens up. Then the landscape runs underneath the bridge and becomes another defined court area at the living room.

AB: Because of the way it curls up on itself, the design also breaks through the traditional sequence of public and private. It doesn't seem to have that kind of hierarchy of front to back, public to private, formal to informal. Everything is formal, everything is public, if you will.

SS: The hierarchy really is about going from the public street side, which is mostly solid except for a few occasional lookout points, to the private inner side and the pool, which is entirely glass. The house itself is a shield from the a cul-de-sac on which it sits. It is solid to the street and then opens up towards the back and the view, where it is entirely transparent.

AARON BETSKY is a critic living in Philadelphia. Previously, he was Director of the School of Architecture and Design at Virginia Tech and President of the School of Architecture at Taliesin. Mr. Betsky is the author of over twenty books on those subjects. He writes a once-weekly blog for architectmagazine.com, Beyond Buildings. Trained as an architect and in the humanities at Yale University, Mr. Betsky has served as the Director of the Cincinnati Art Museum (2006-2014) and the Netherlands Architecture Institute (2001-2006), as well as Curator of Architecture and Design at the San Francisco Museum of Modern Art (1995-2001). In 2008, he also directed the 11th Venice International Biennale of Architecture. His latest books are *Fifty Lessons from Frank Lloyd Wright* (2021), *Making It Modern* (2019), *Architecture Matters* (2019) and *Anarchitecture: The Monster Leviathan*.

AB: You worked really, really hard to make the house appear to float as much as you could. Why was that so important?

SS: I'm interested in the ephemeralization of architecture. The fact that the clients are tech people that live in an electronic world where the object has shrunk to the minimum made it seem appropriate. I wanted to make a house that was part of that era of immateriality and objectlessness, to diminish its presence as much as possible; to make it as invisible as possible. Through this threading around the house, almost everything other than the wall on the street completely dissolves itself. It's not about an inside and outside. It's about continuity. It is Miesian [based on the work of the German architect Ludwig Mies van der Rohe], but more so, in a sculptural way. Within that drive, the design is about the compression of the mechanics of the home. That then allows for the expansion of free space. The result is a set of elements that accumulate functions such as the living room, kitchen and dining, and the bedrooms into bars, separated by pods that punctuate the bars and make the spaces function in particular, different ways.

AB: Those last elements, like the kitchen, have all their accoutrements, but they are all played down, if not repressed, so that they become modules made up of different degrees of solids and voids. There's an extreme reduction of the architectural vocabulary here, right?

SS: I think you also have to see it as part of a modernist tradition, and a particular one that is important to where the house sits in California. Specifically, that is a residential modernist history that has to do with the Case Study program houses [of Arts & Architecture Magazine in the 1950s and 1960s], the Eichler houses [created by the developer of that name during the same period], and the whole tradition of modernity in Northern California, which had quite a robust period in the 1950s and 1960s. I think that all the way up into the early 1970s there were actually very beautiful modern buildings built here – before Post Modernism arrived. I want the house to be seen as part of a California legacy and typology, that started with [the work of] [Rudolf] Schindler and [Richard] Neutra and crystallized after the war in the work of Pierre Koenig and the Case Study houses, as well as the work of Charles and Ray Eames

AB: So it was all the fault of Post Modernism? What about the equally robust Bay Area School and its emphasis on modernism built with local materials and a sense of the local landscape, which was also true for the Eichler homes?

SS: There was always a strong tradition of steel and glass and, yes, wood, but it was modernist, it was reductive, influenced by Japan.

AB: If that is true, that also gives the house a certain placelessness, because it could be in Timbuktu or, rather, in Southern California. The location wouldn't change either the materiality or the interior definition of the project.

SS: It would have to be modified, as it has been designed this way because of the relation to the street and the view.

AB: It is also a single-family version of the systems you have developed for your multi-unit residential structures, which are made up of repetitive modules and grids.

SS: It is definitely modeled on the idea of making free space that is a as neutral as possible, to give the owners the opportunity to particularize that space.

AB: You have taken it further here, though. In your recent work, visible details and service spaces have disappeared. They are hard to find in this house. Even the staircases have been suppressed.

SS: It is about de-objectifying the object and making it like a computer. All the internal stuff that's going on in the computer isn't visible. The same is true here. The detailing on this house is very definitely worked on. If you look at the building sections you can see how we buried the vent pipes in the depth of the roof, or the way the window spans to the top of the roof line, creating a pocket for a shade. It's about creating an object without noise, but those details are quite difficult to accomplish. It's not that I'm not obsessed with the details, but it's just that I want to make them silent. I always try to describe my work in terms of it being more of a framework than an object, more an instrument than a monument.

AB: This seems to be getting to the point where it's the framework that, like Ouroboros, the mythical snake eating its tail, which Oz House also resembles, is starting to eat itself, right? It's starting to disappear into itself.

SS: I would say that's probably true. But, you know, the ultimate goal has always been to create frameworks of opportunity. It is to de-program, instead of programming as it is common in architecture: eliminating that whole idea of what architecture does that programs people. Instead it actually provides opportunity. It frees occupants to create their world.

AB: Like [the artist] Sol LeWitt's cubes?

SS: Yes, like Sol LeWitt's cubes. That sort of minimalist art is very important to me. I have some Donald Judd prints in my house that I look at every day when I shower. They are about the same kind of unfolding, of dissolving and recombining in different ways, very much like the two "L" shapes that make up this house.

AB: But, to be honest, there is a sense that the house is also a demonstration of the scale and nature of wealth in the degree to which it pushes its abstraction.

SS: The client pretty much drove that. The first layout of this house was something like 11,000 square feet of space and it had most of the accommodation that they needed. But they kept on expanding their needs. For example, the basement was initially a small thing. It ended up being the entire footprint of one of the Ls.

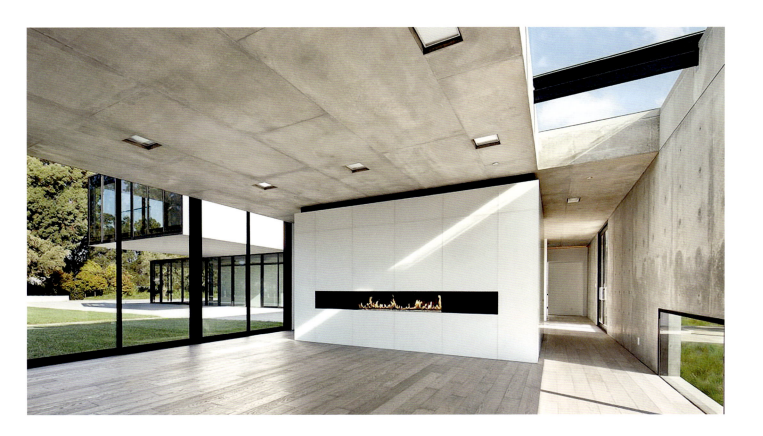

AB: One of the things I noted was you kept it abstract even at that scale. It took me time to find the staircases.

SS: They are there, and they are actually quite beautiful.

AB: But their invisibility seems very deliberate. I think that, if you could, you would like to teleport people between floors.

SS: That would actually be quite good.

AB: So what you wind up with is a single organizational piece with objects floating inside of it. The repeated bar is a typological and organizational mediator between the repetitive framework and the realities of site and program and character or the people living there, right?

SS: Yes, that's it. But it is also meant to amplify the qualities of the site, to expand and enhance the found. It is meant to make the clients happy by giving them things that provide pleasure and improve the way that life works for them. They keep telling me about the discovery of the way things like light work in the bars, or how views and connections appear. It creates a world of fascination and discovery. Sometimes the simplest things actually have the most potent realities. That, I think, is part of what one wants to give to the owners.

AB: That is what you gave the owners. What about the house's responsibility to sustainability?

SS: It has to do with the economy of means and ends. This stripped down minimalism is actually about a rigorous use of resources. An example is how the window system is completely repetitive: there's only one type in the whole building. So, by shrinking the structure's complexity and creating a systematic set of elements we created an economy of repetition.

AB: And what does it do in terms of its context, both in time and place?

SS: I think about that continually. It has do with continuity and transformation. I see my task as being able to take from tradition and reinvigorate it with the present. I do see this house as accomplishing a certain amount of that. It does root itself in a tradition that we've already talked about, but then it also takes it to a more contemporary moment, which is this set of ideas of the ephemeralization of the object and the kind of reduction of that object to the most extreme degree possible.

AB: And, finally, what does it do for architecture?

SS: What's the responsibility of architecture? It is, among other things, to feed the next generation of architects. I like to see the design of the Oz House in a continuum of experiments and building spaces that are appropriate to California. I would like somehow for this to add something to that, and for the next generation of architects to maybe include this in their own string of ideas.

DESIGN

DESCRIPTION
BY STANLEY SAITOWITZ

The site is a hilltop in Atherton, accessed via the winding Ridgeview Drive, ending in a circular cul de sac. The entry gate is framed by a concrete wall from which the house number, 96, is incised. Once inside, views unfold, and the entry canopy, floating above a pool, frames the bay and skyline of San Francisco in the distance.

L shaped bars of space lace the site, measuring the topography without interrupting the terrain, like cartography describing the land. On the side facing the cul de sac and neighbors, the bars are solid and concrete, on the side opening to the views, glass and open.

These L shaped bars balance on top of each other creating courts and overhangs, defining indoor and outdoor spaces with bridges and cantilevers.

Services are solid elements which comb the space with pods of mechanism and storage floating within the open lines of the bars.

The basement is for family play and casual entertaining opening to a large grassed area. A light court carved into the ground illuminates the other side of the L. Above is the main level for formal entertaining which cantilevers over the basement and looks out on the city view. Dining, kitchen and family areas are in the other leg of the L, where stairs go up to the bedroom L, inverted and floating above. The leg facing the city view is the master, cantilevered over the wing below to create an outdoor room, the other leg contains four children's suites, connected by an office, sitting area and laundry that bridge a void below.

The bars open to different directions of the hilltop, with views of treetops, the bay and the city.

The residence is a reduced expression of sheer material and form where connections and intersections are minimized to non-existence.

The building threads and weaves, making holes in things, or making things that make holes in things that are not, doubling the spaces of opportunity. The bars twist and fold, cross and loop, bridge and divide. At the intersections are vertical connections. These abstract geologies do not impose, but expose, expanding the realm of space and diminishing the role of form.

The interest is in transparency and lightness contrasted with solidity and mass, folding on themselves, slipping and sliding through space as they frame and connect.

PRESENTATION DRAWINGS

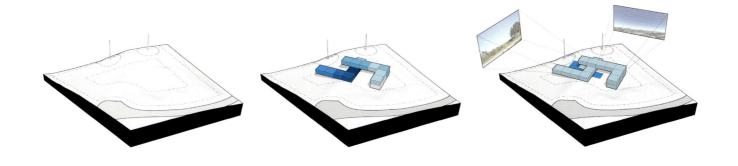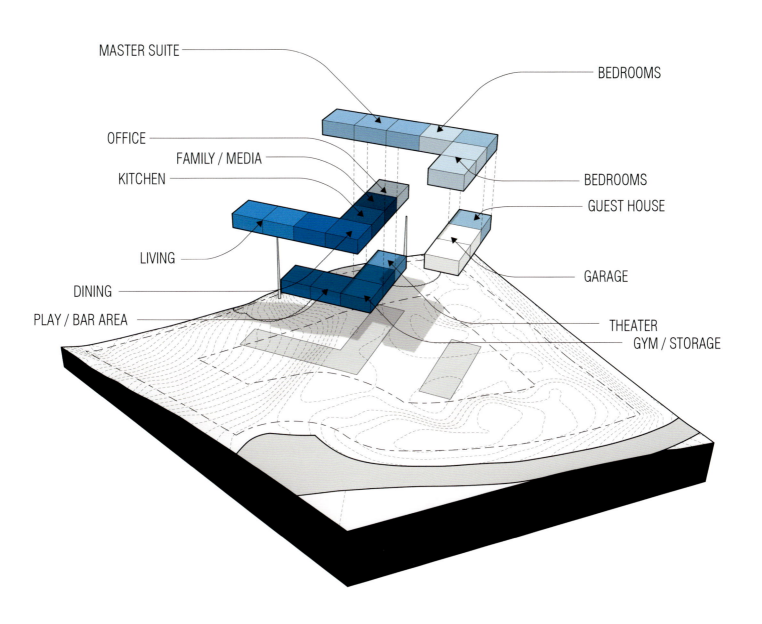

Siteplan

024 | DESIGN / PRESENTATION DRAWINGS

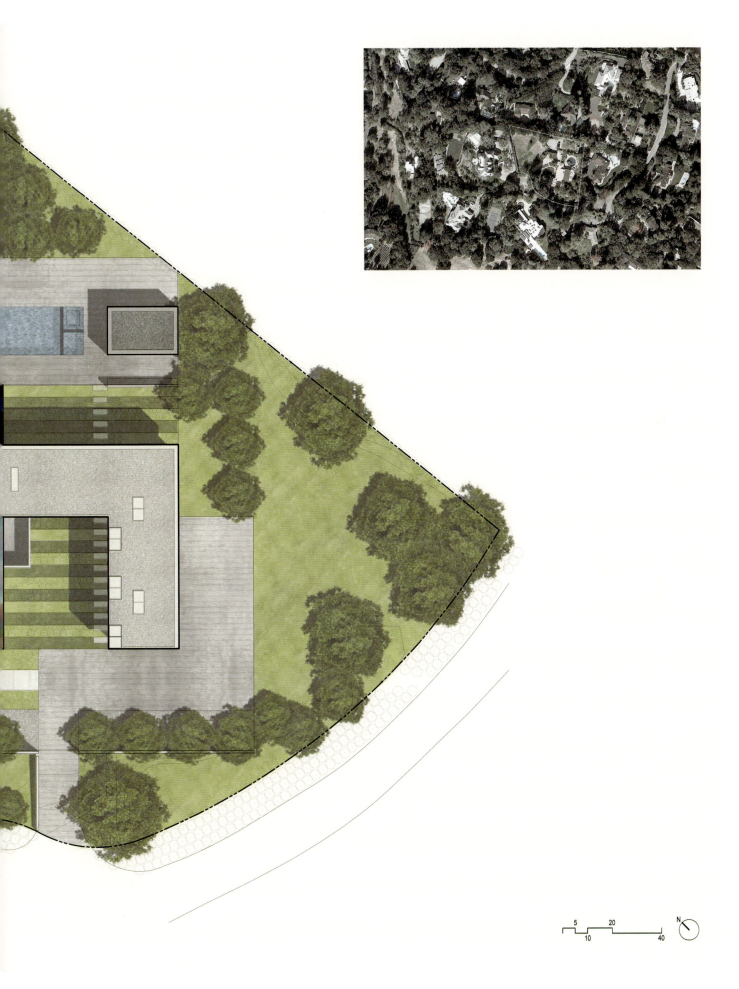

Second Floor Plan

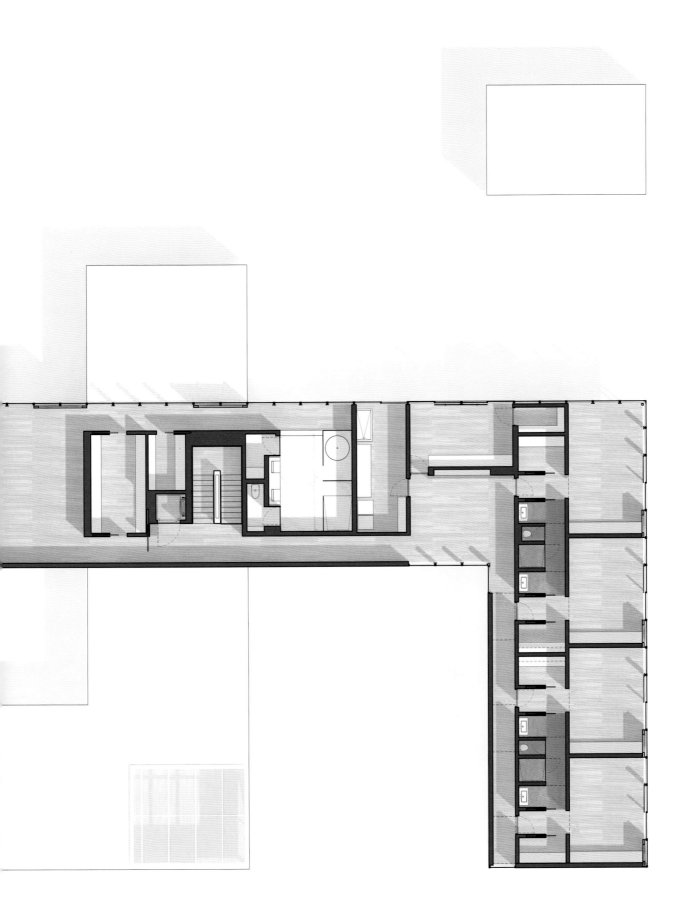

027

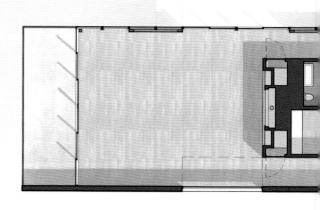

First Floor Plan

028 | DESIGN / PRESENTATION DRAWINGS

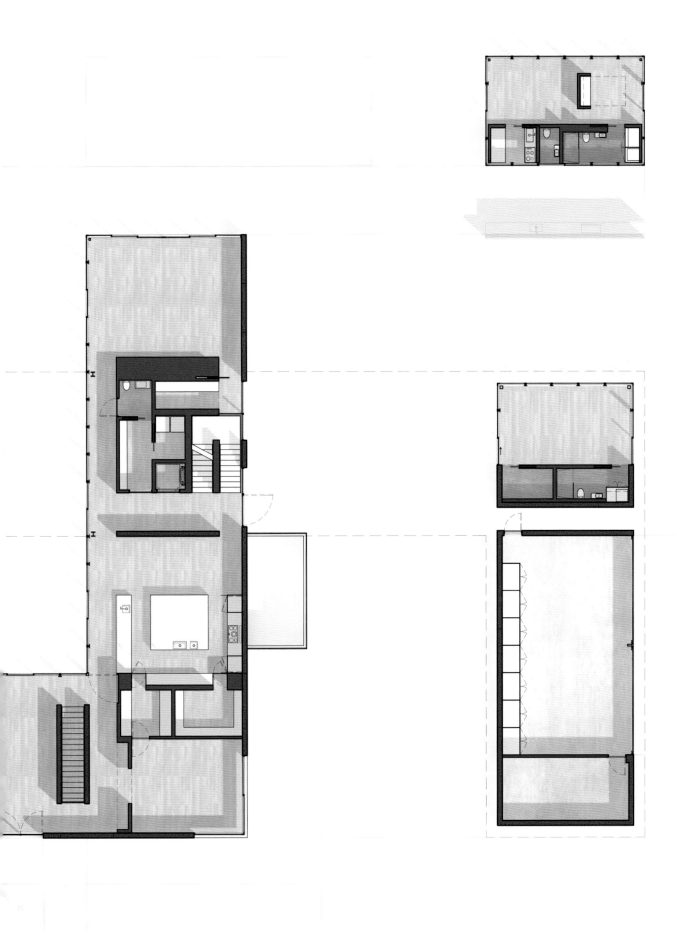

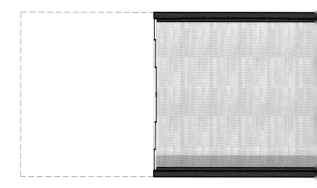

Basement Floor Plan

030 | DESIGN / PRESENTATION DRAWINGS

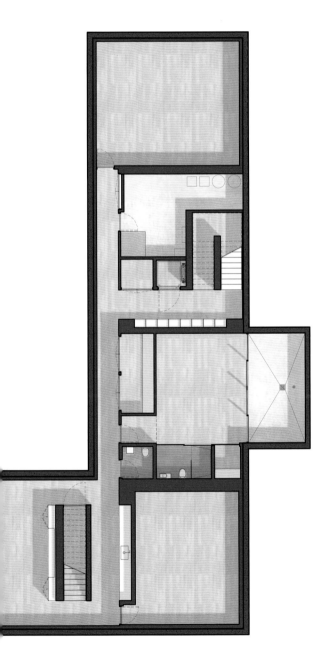

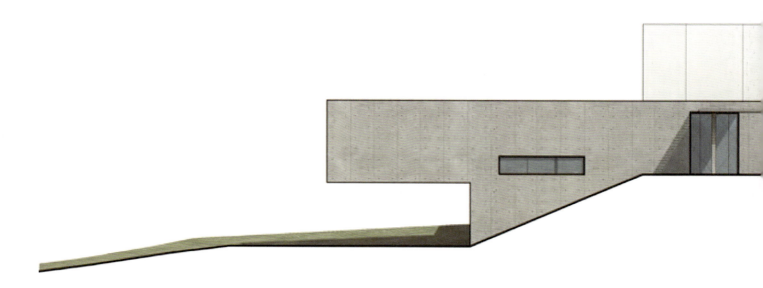

South Elevation

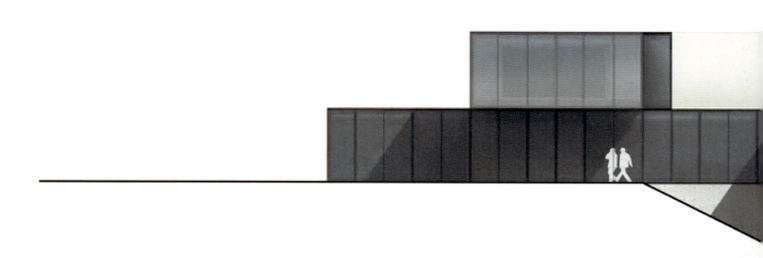

West Elevation

032 | DESIGN / PRESENTATION DRAWINGS

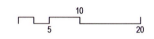
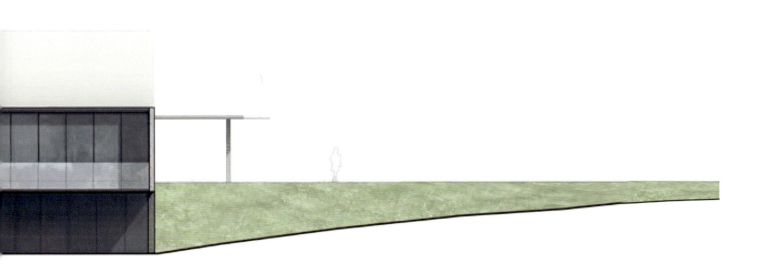

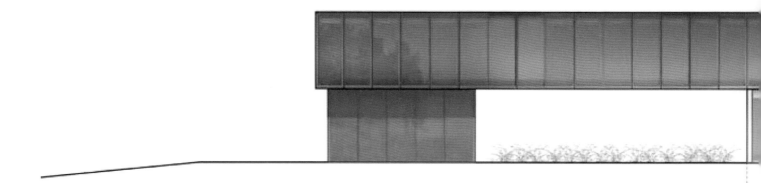

North Elevation

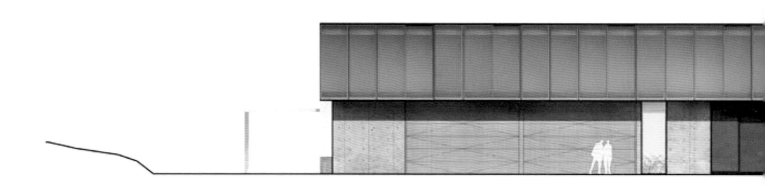

East Elevation

034 | DESIGN / PRESENTATION DRAWINGS

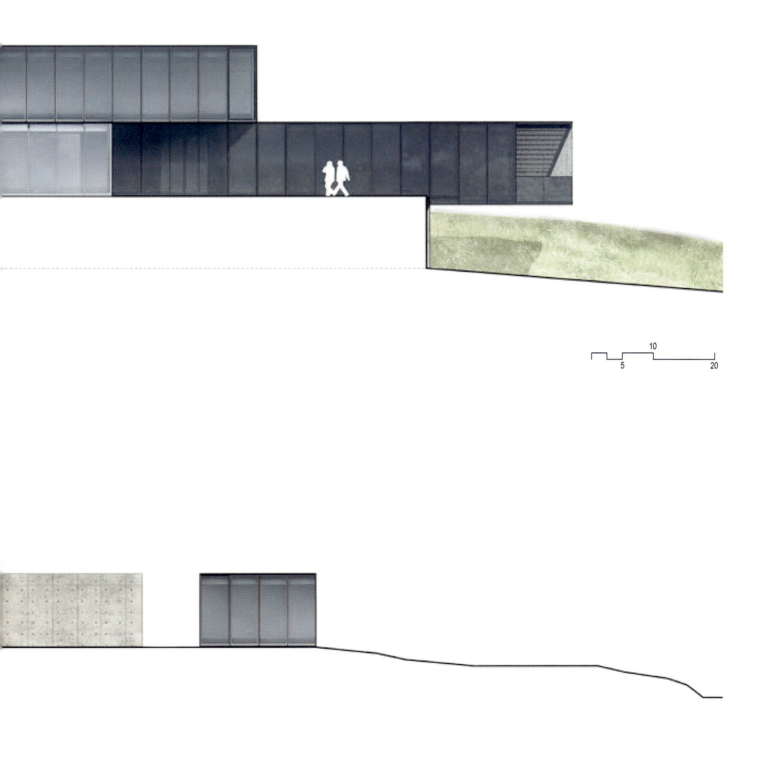

038 | DESIGN / PRESENTATION DRAWINGS

CONSTRUCTION

WORKING DRAWINGS

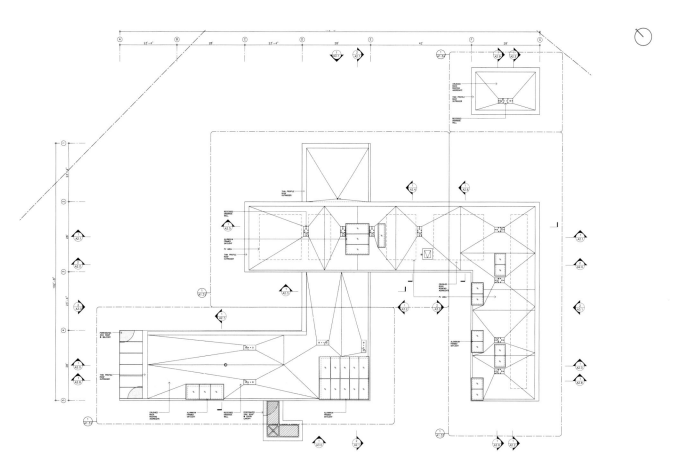

Roof plan

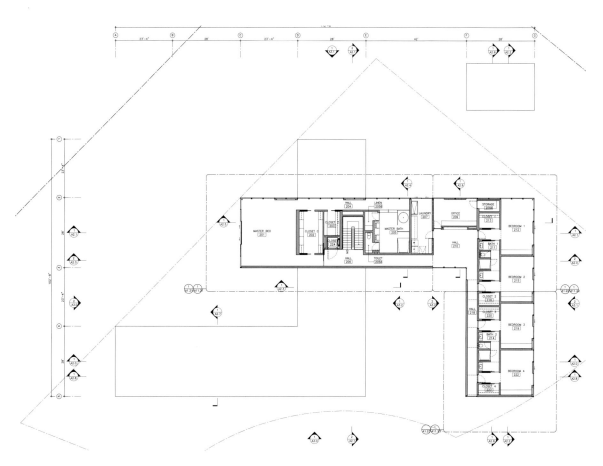

Upper level plan

047

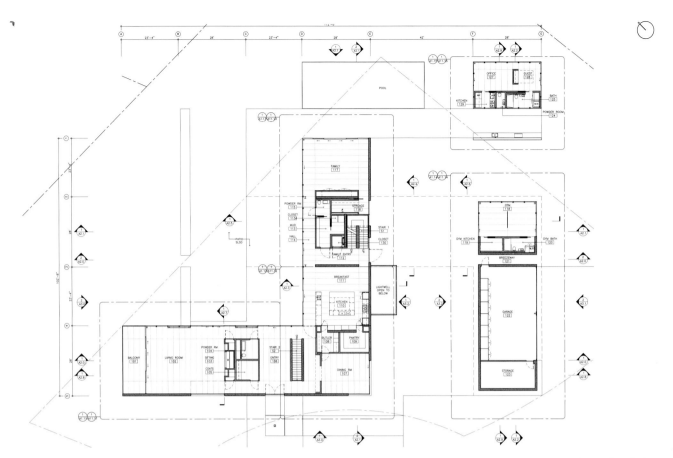

Lower level plan

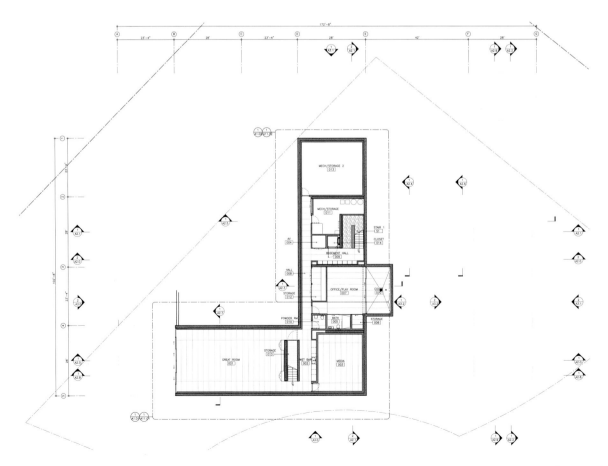

Basement level plan

048 | CONSTRUCTION / WORKING DRAWINGS

Sections

049

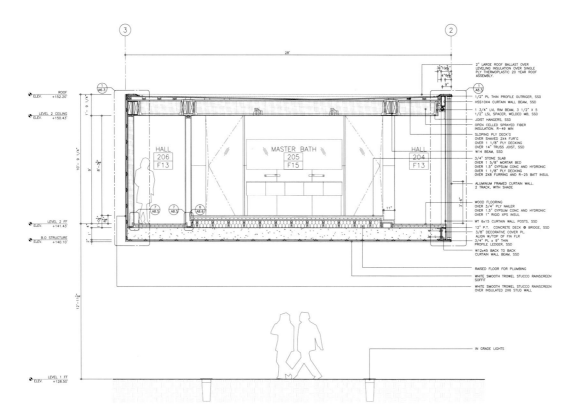

Detail building section. Bridge and Master Bedroom

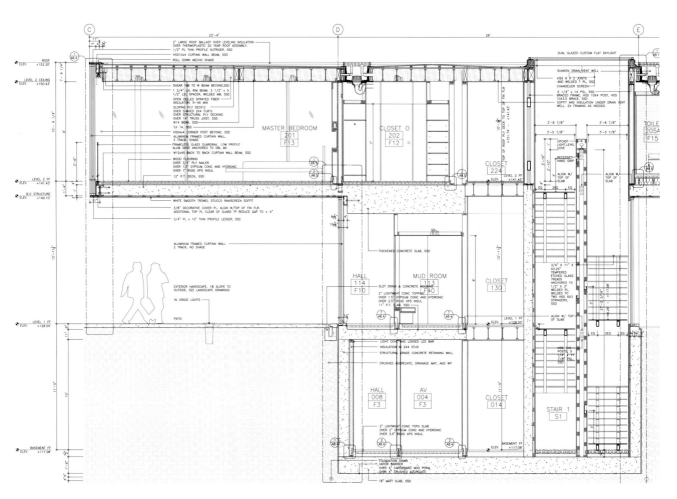

Detail building section. Elevator and Master Bedroom

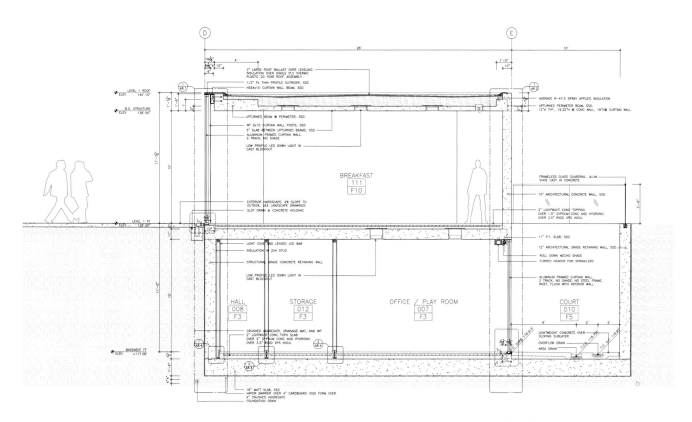

Detail building section. Court and family room

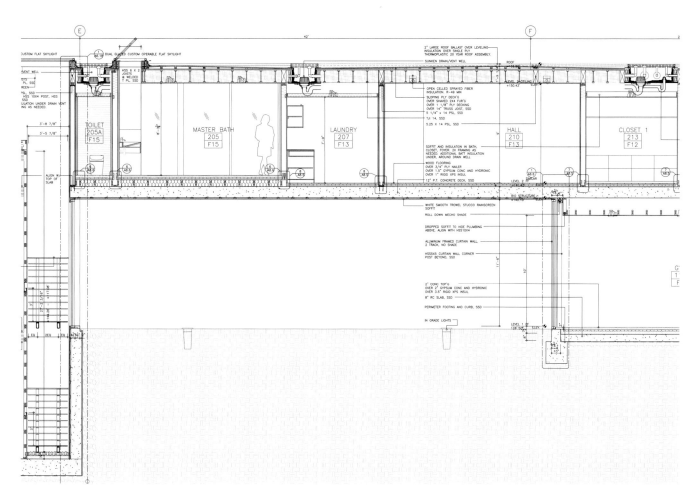

Detail building section. Bridge and common space

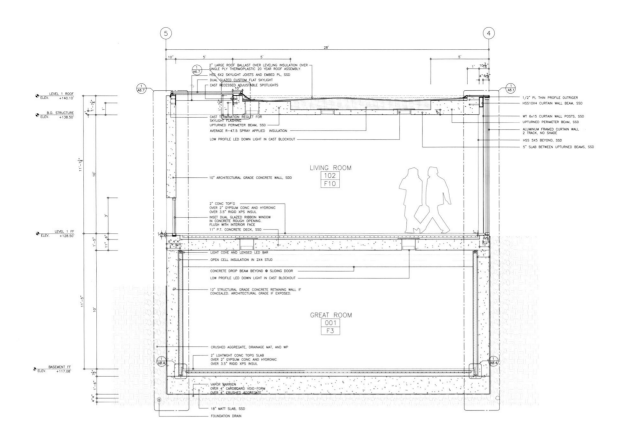

Detail building section. Living room

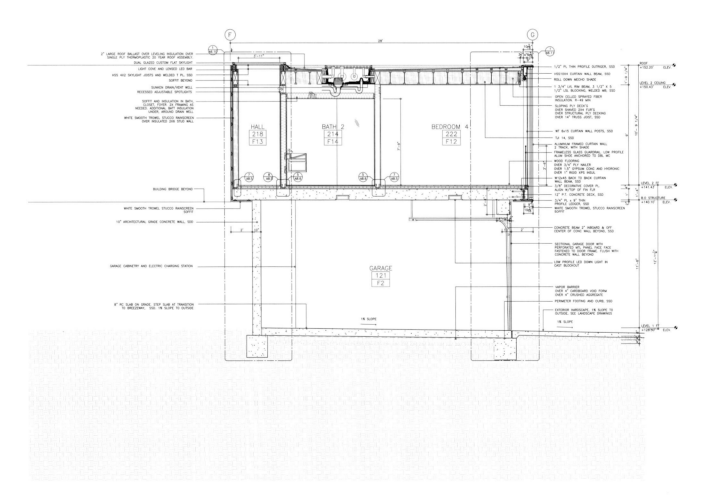

Detail building section. Garage and Bedroom

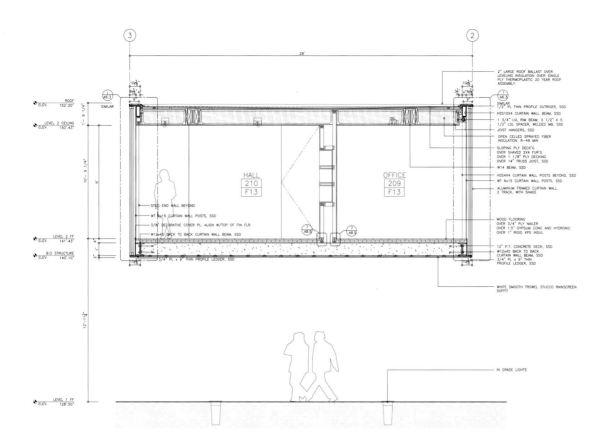

Detail building section. Common room bridge

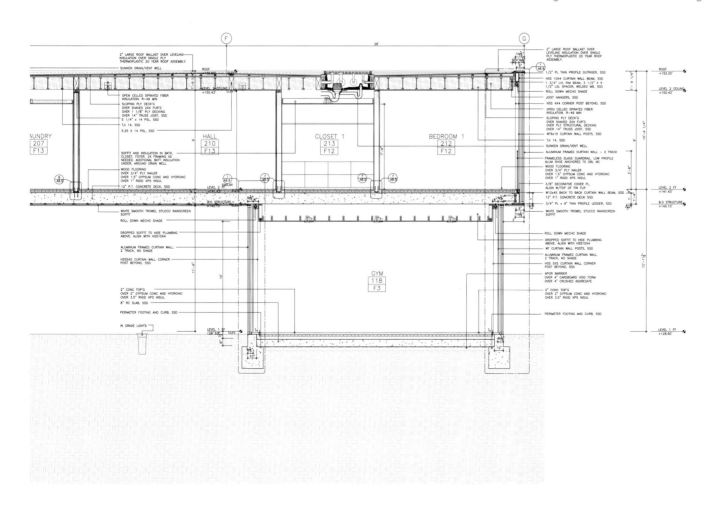

Detail building section. Bedroom and guest house

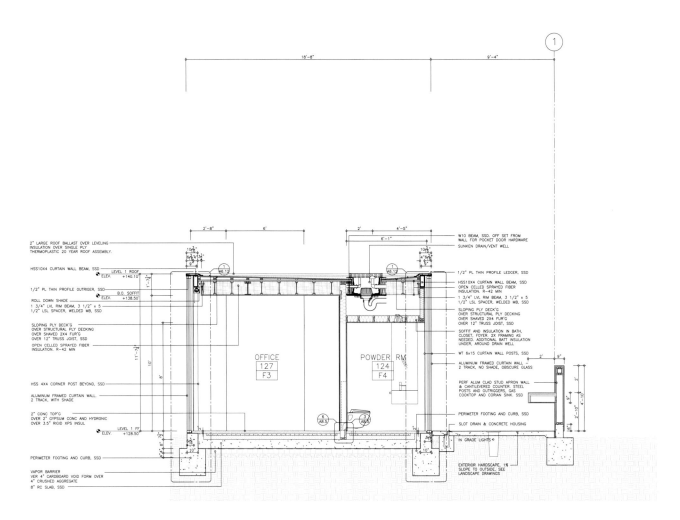

Detail building section. Accessory structure

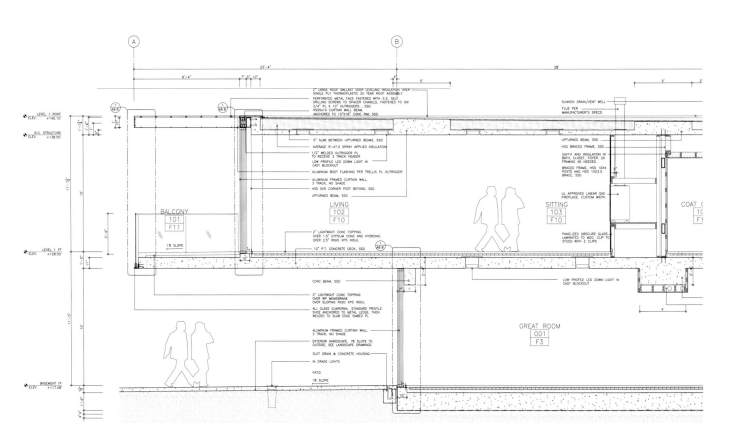

Detail building section. Living room balcony and great room

054 | CONSTRUCTION / WORKING DRAWINGS

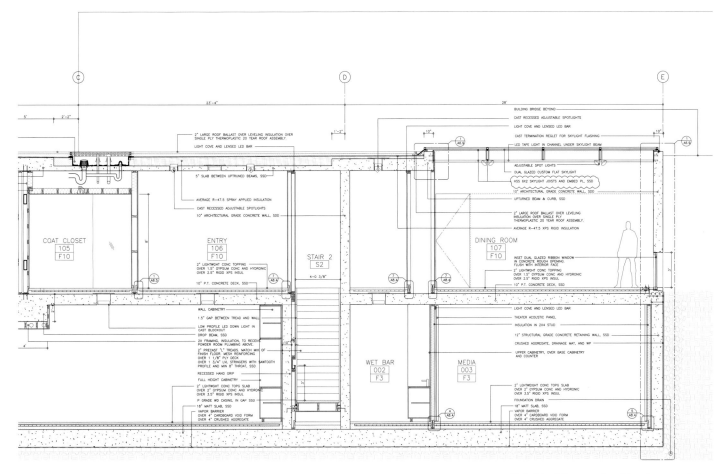

Detail building section. Theater and dining

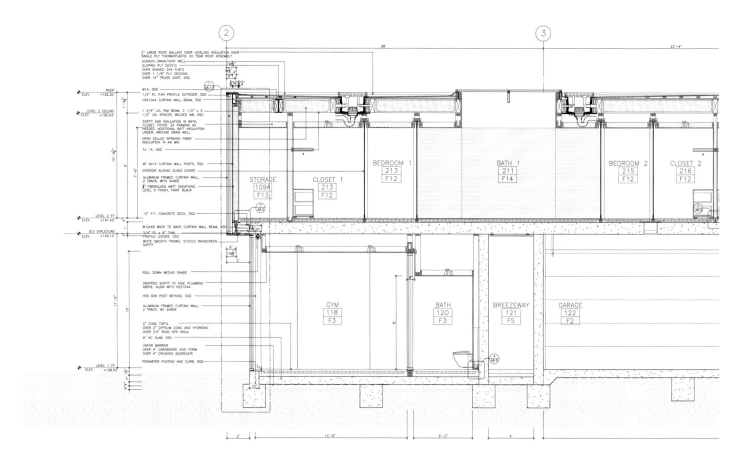

Detail building section. Gym, Garage and Bedrooms

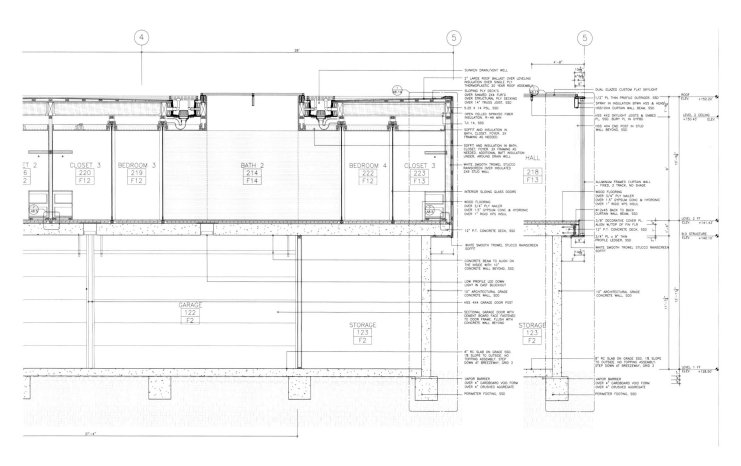

Detail building section. Garage and Bedrooms

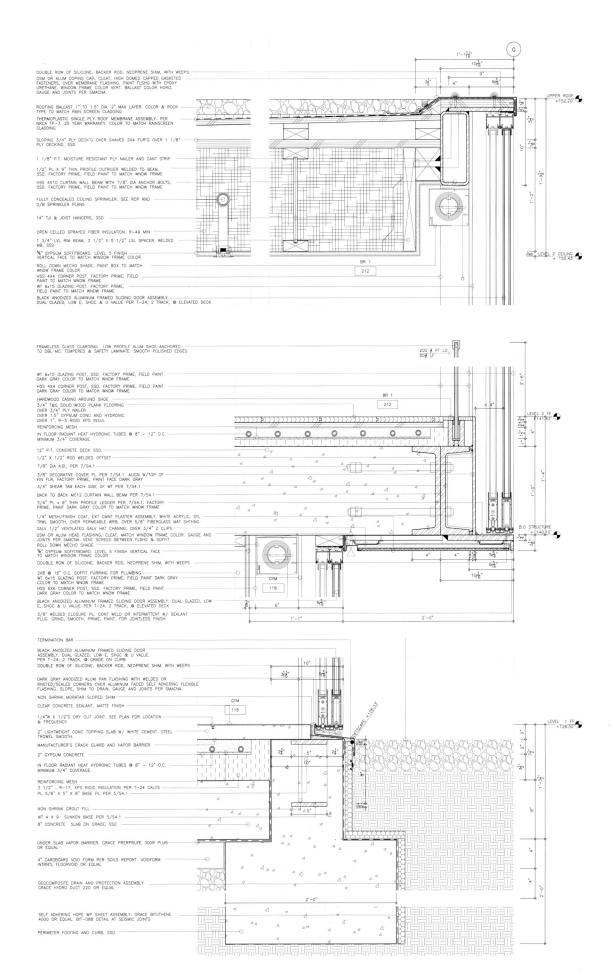

Detail Building Section Gym

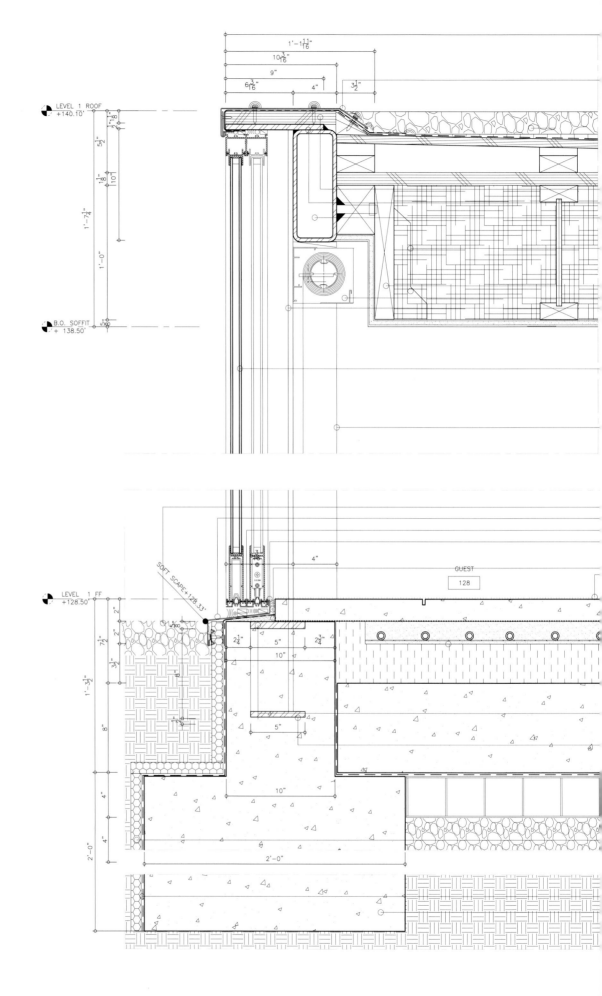

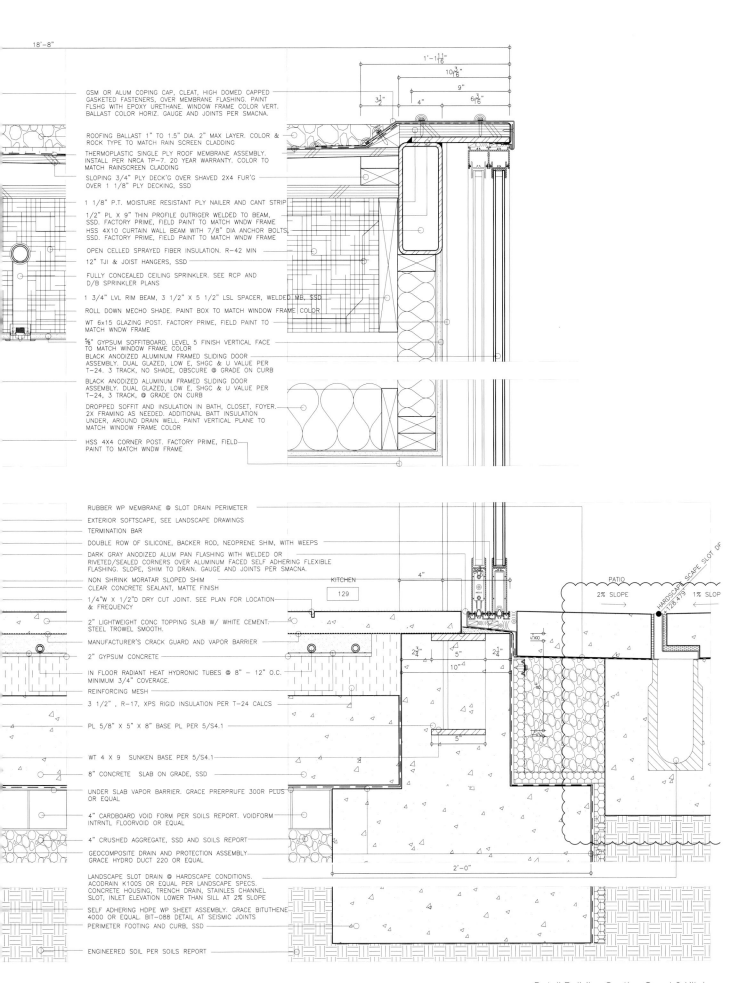

Detail Building Section Guest & Kitchen

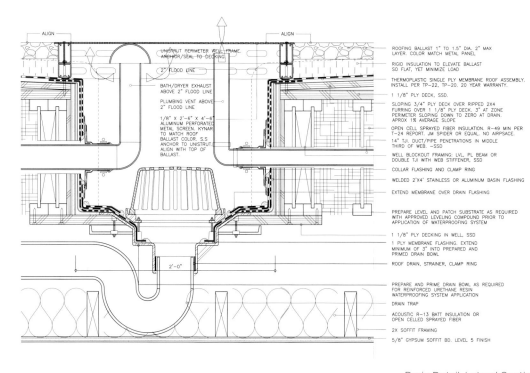

Drain Detail. Lateral Section

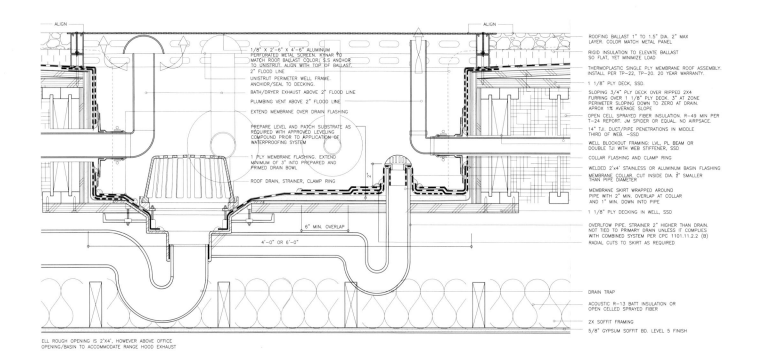

Drain Detail. Longitudinal Section

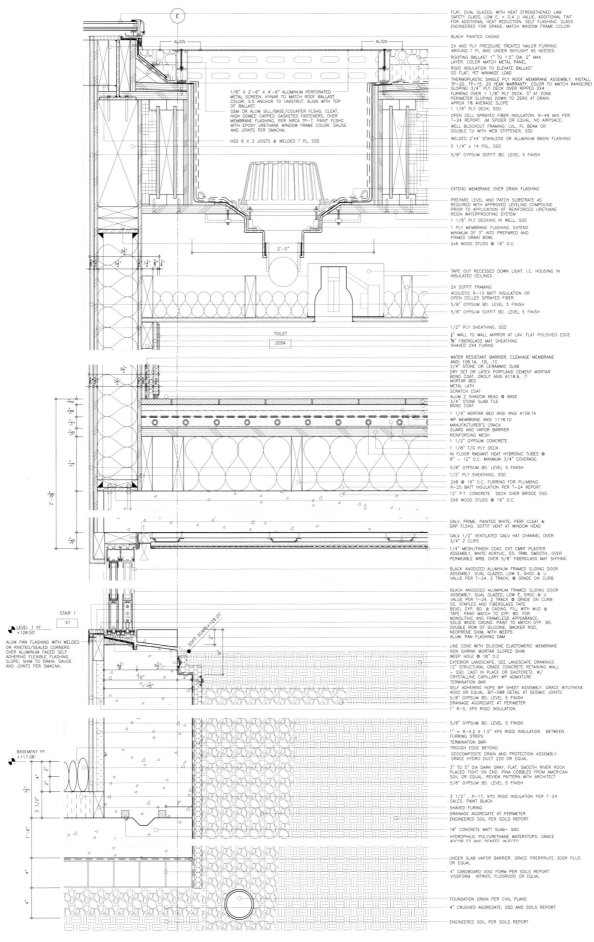

Detail Building Section Toilet

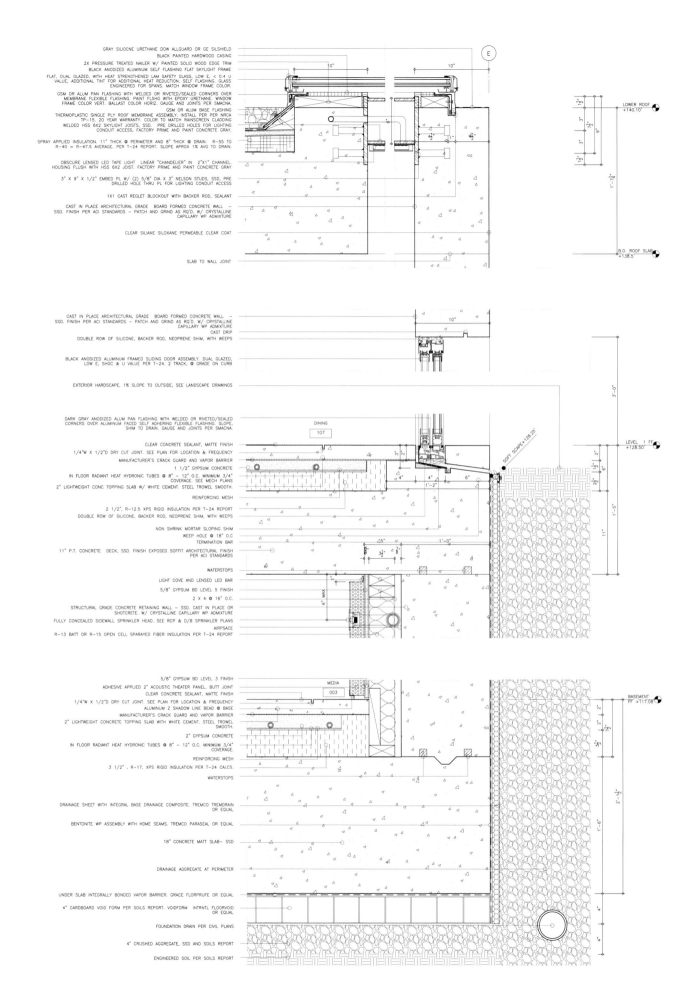

Detail Building Section Dining & Media

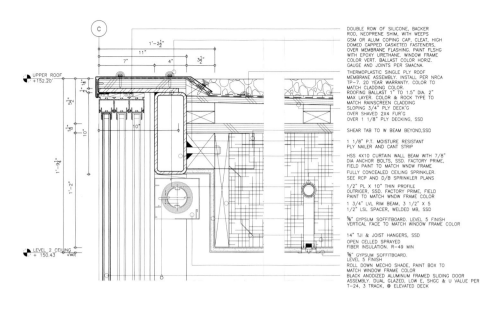
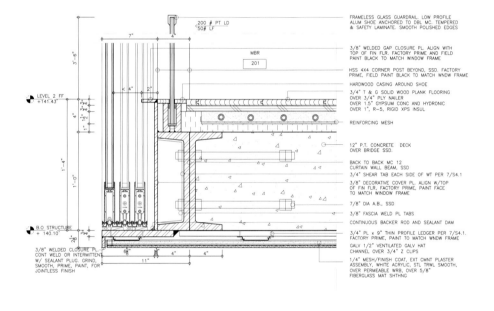
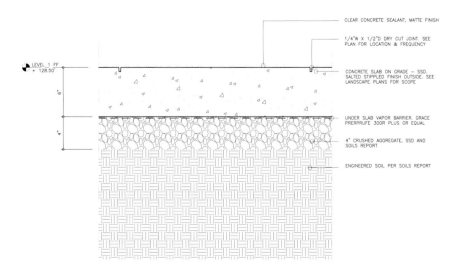

Detail Building Section
Master Bedroom

063

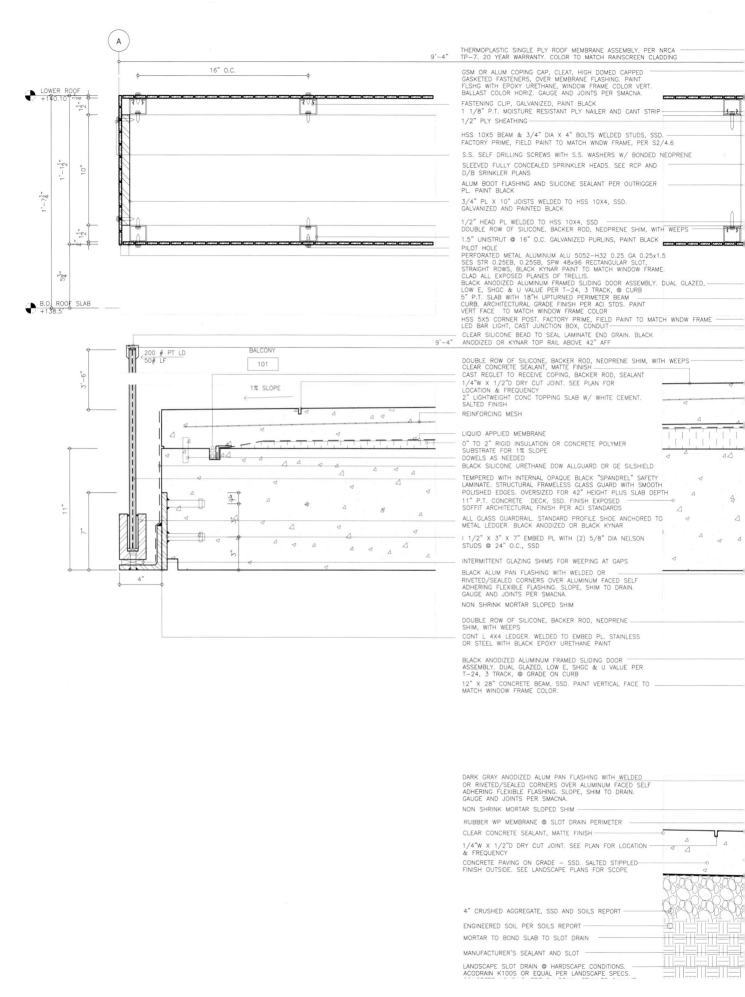

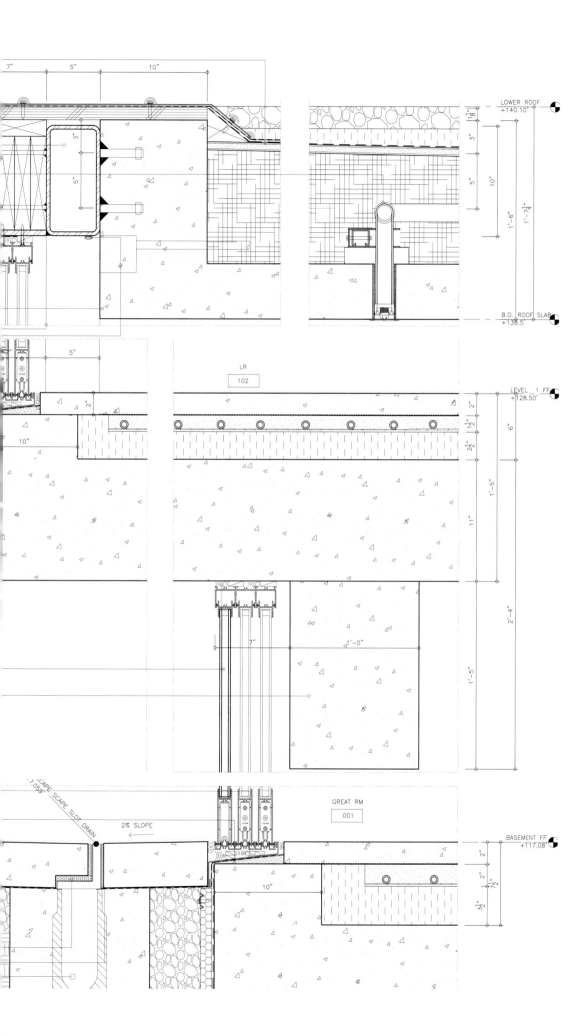

Detail Building Section
Balcony & Great Room

065

PROCESS

068 | CONSTRUCTION

070 | CONSTRUCTION / PROCESS

072 | CONSTRUCTION / PROCESS

074 | CONSTRUCTION / PROCESS

080 | CONSTRUCTION / PROCESS

086 | CONSTRUCTION / PROCESS

090 | CONSTRUCTION / PROCESS

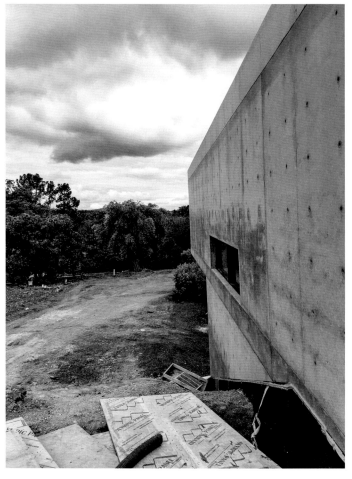

094 | CONSTRUCTION / PROCESS

BUILDING

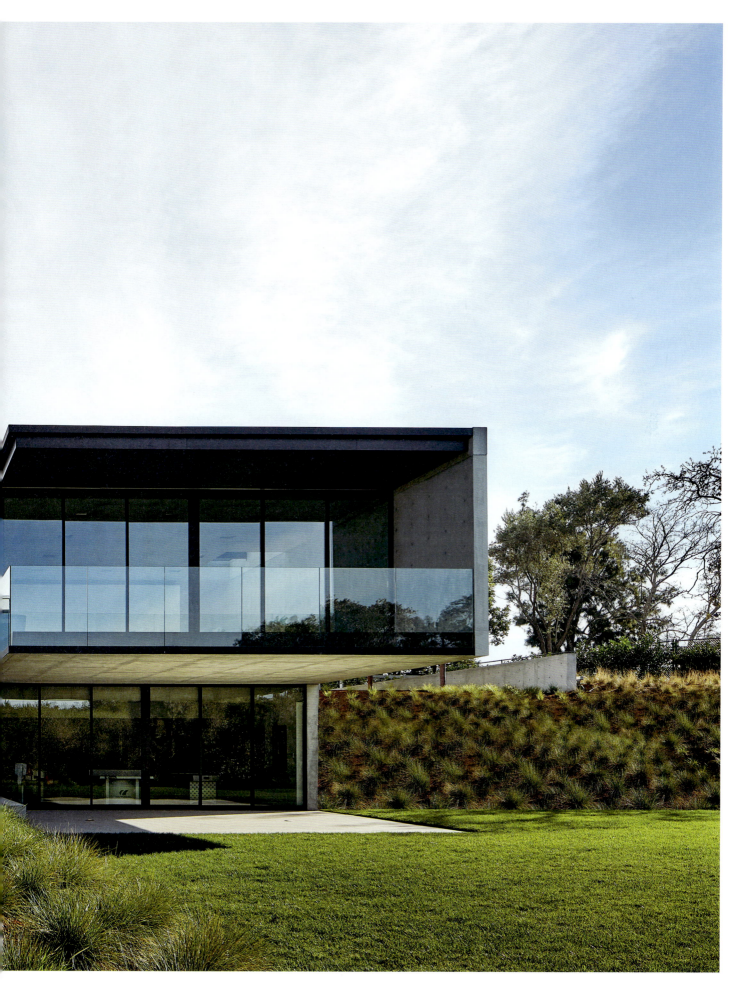

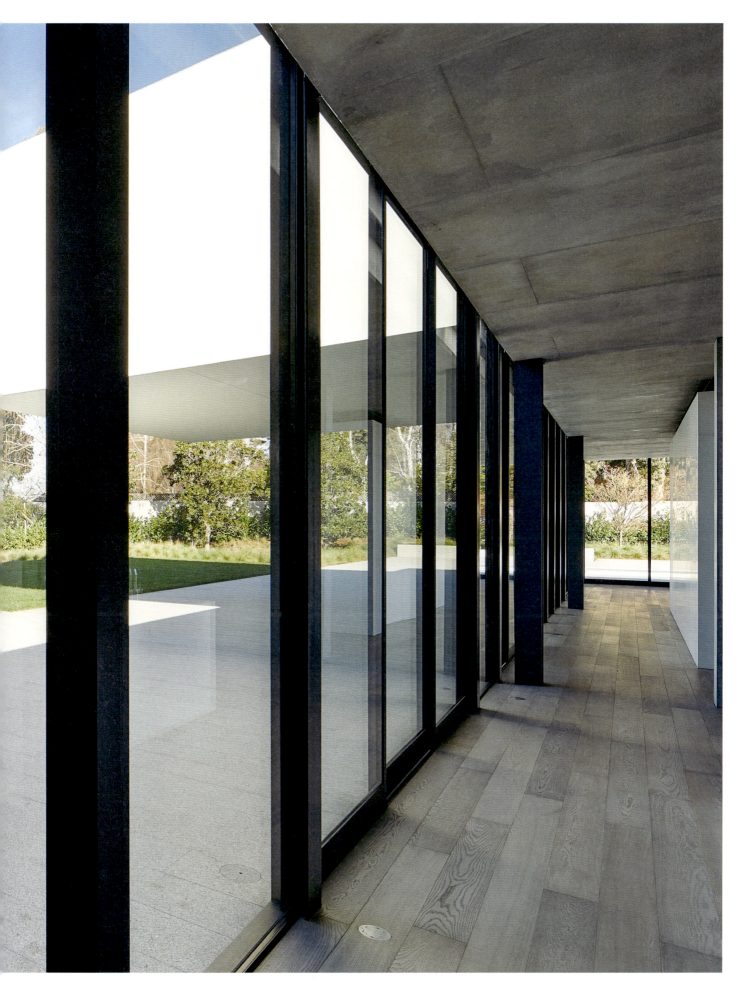

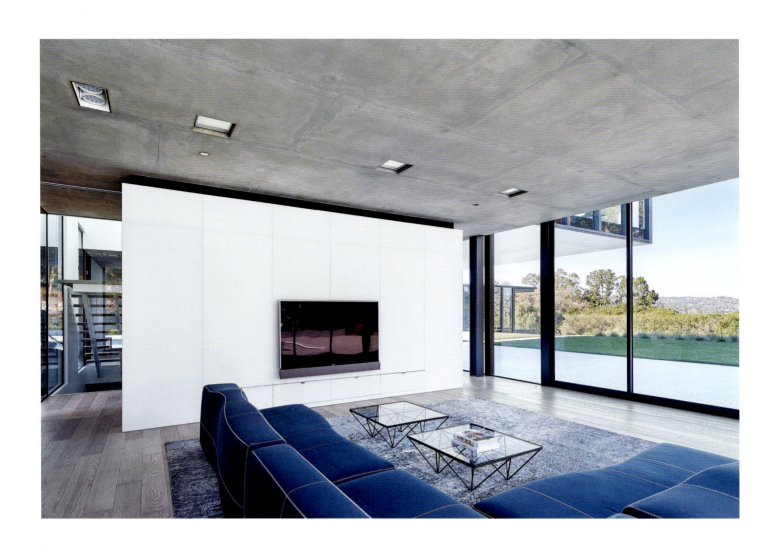

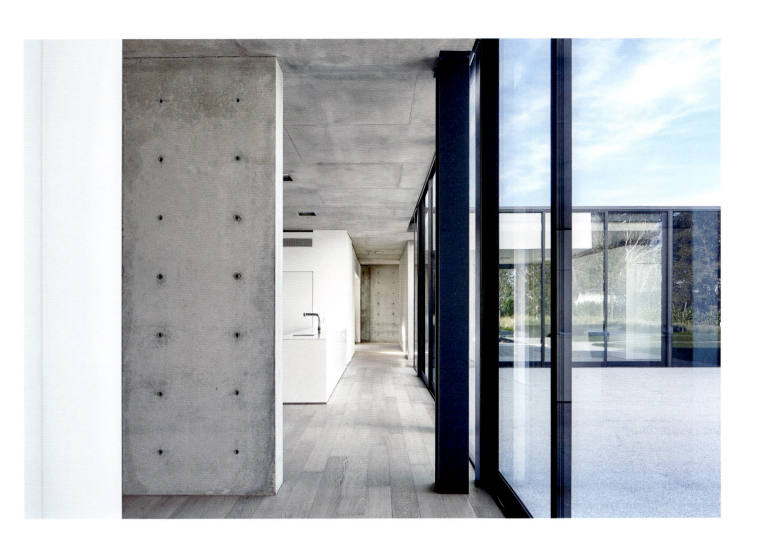

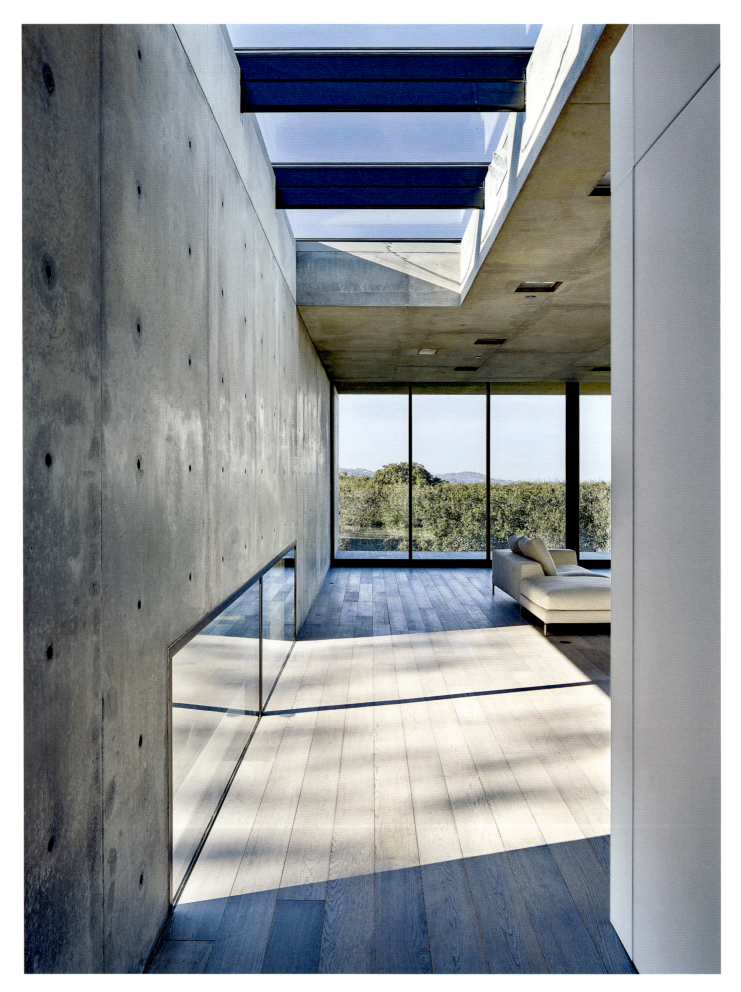

130 | BUILDING

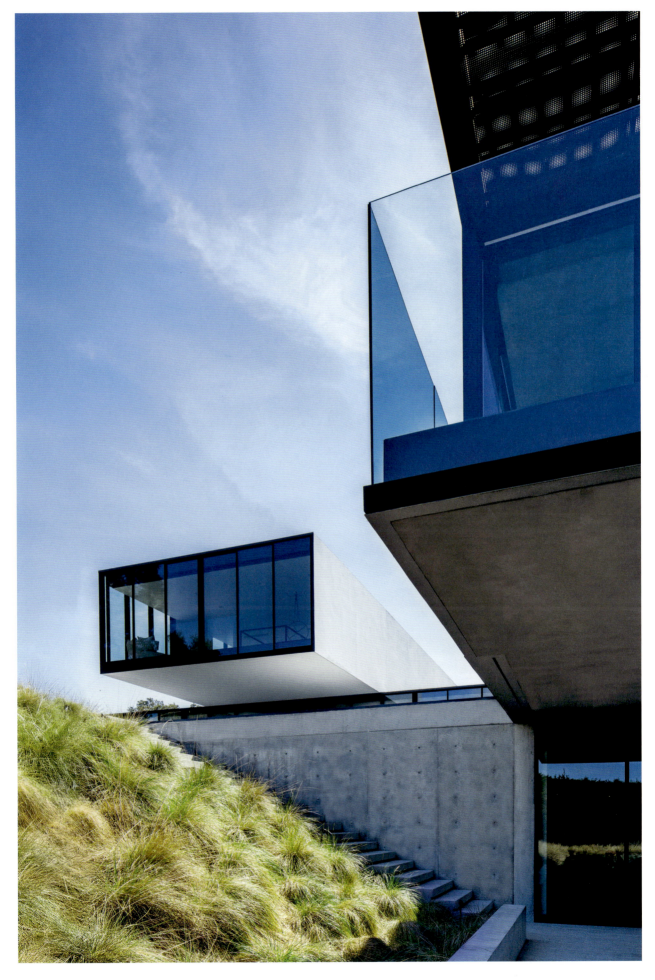

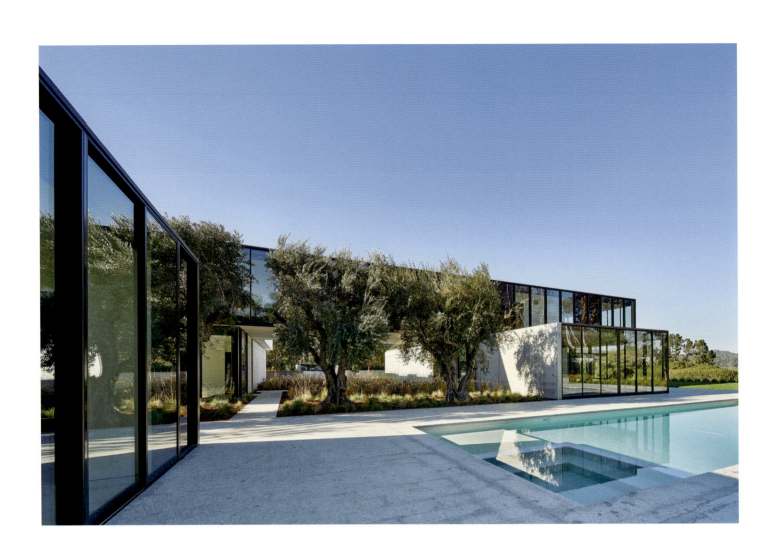

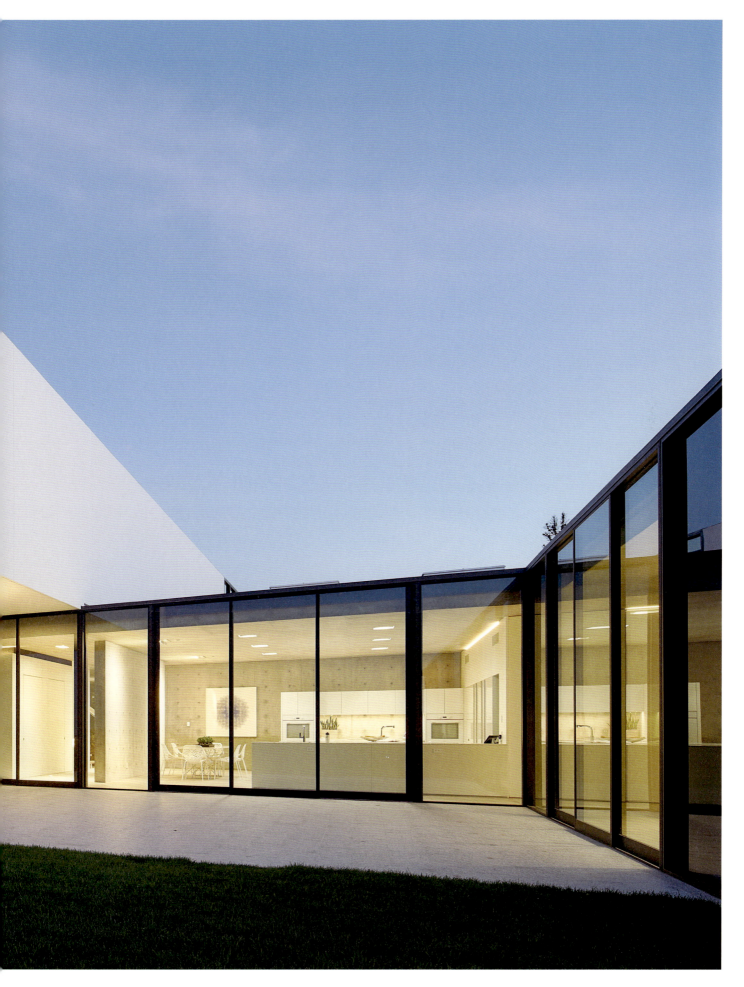

EPILOGUE

BAR HOUSES
BY STANLEY SAITOWITZ

1

The journey to the Oz House has been long, with many forking paths.

Looking back I now see the steps, one by one, from the earliest houses in landscapes, to DiNapoli in Los Gatos, the first house arranged in a pair of walls. The site was a promontory which the two bars of program edged and protected as a series of courts, the central one enclosed as the living room pavilion. The house emerged to track and conserve the landscape. (Images 1, 2, 3)

2

3

4

5

6

Rabin is the first house David Warner, Red Horse Constructors and I worked on together, more than 30 years ago, in Tiburon. The house is a long bar, cranked at the center, that tracks the contours and continues as a series of terraces dissolving into the landscape and focused on the view of the bay below. (Images 4, 5, 6) At the center is a void, bridged by the family room above, that frames the view at the entry.

7

The Byron Meyer house in Sonoma is a radiating bar which ties together the three geographies of the site; a hill, a valley and a promontory. The building comprises three structures: An entertainment house, a master suite, and a guest wing. These are joined by two bars, a bridge, and a porch, linking the buildings through the landscape. As the buildings slide through the geography, they tie the elements of terrain together. (Images 7, 8, 9)

8

9

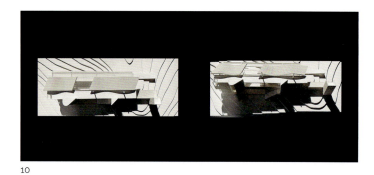

10

The Laz Beach house begins as a wall, parallel to the bluff and the waves, a wall that stabilizes the plan, a wall that is the spine of services, a wall that holds the light glass shack together, a wall that longs to support the bluff. Along this wall, the space of the beach house is divided into two rooms, one for living and eating, one for sleeping. Between these rooms is an outdoor living court. Along the ocean side of the house a continuous porch touches the top of the dune and leads to the beach. (Image 10)

11

Lieff continues these linear arrangements in landscapes. The house is a long bar with two carved courts, one for the entry, the other between living and master suite. The Corten steel wall is a mechanical spine, separated by clerestory lighting from the mostly glass interior. The spaces of habitation extend towards the view, shaded and focused with stucco walls which form an arcade and expand the interior to the view. (Images 11, 12, 13)

12

13

174 | EPILOGUE

14

The first design for Zakin is where the idea of the Bar Houses first emerged. The site is above the Silverado Trail with a broad panorama of the Napa Valley.

The house is two 20' wide L shaped bars, one placed on the other, forming a courtyard. The entry is a procession from the auto court, under the floating bar, across the court, into the living bar. The lower L has the public, family and guest quarters.

The upper L are bedrooms, with the master suite occupying one leg, and the children's wing the other. Within the bars, lateral walls of services and storage comb the space into various functional units. The bars were constructed out of post tensioned concrete decks, supporting glass and concrete walls.

At the intersections of the two L shaped bars, the overlap becomes vertical circulation within the two-story volumes.

A linear pool reflects the adjacent bar. After budgeting, this design was abandoned for a single story set of bars. (Images 14, 15)

15

16

17

18

176 | EPILOGUE

19

The built Zakin is approached from the north, a long bar with two wings attached forming three spaces; a car yard; a central entry court; and a garden for the master suite.

The long bar has a continuous porch overlooking the Napa Valley on the south. This bar is in turn divided by two courtyards into three areas; the library and formal living spaces; the kitchen and family room; and the study and master suite. The two wings which extend from the bar contain the garages and theatre on the east, and the children's bedrooms on the west.

Sliding glass walls enclose the kitchen and family room on two sides, making the house a transparent frame through which the landscape continues from courtyard to valley. (Images 16, 17, 18, 19)

Windows at the floor float the walls, allowing the space to continue into the water and landscape, and protect the interior.

The house is simple in shape and grand in scale. The single line of the house with its rhythmic columns provides measure to the backdrop of nature. Transparent and reflective surfaces contain and expand.

Below, a long swimming pool, reflecting the house, is dug into the hill and floats above the valley. Redhorse Constructors collaborated on the construction.

20

This is another project with Redhorse Constructors. The Bridge House spans a ravine as a singular 22' wide two story rusted bar, measuring the landscape.

A stair leads up to the entry court. The living areas are the upper level and have continuous glass walls which look north to the spacious hills. The bedrooms below have glass walls that look south to an intimate theater in the landscape.

The top bar is slipped to provide shade for the lower south facing one, and a deck on the north. Skylights balance the light above. (Images 20, 21)

From above and below two opposite experiences of the landscape are focused; broad and expansive from the upper level; defined and enclosed below.

21

22

Along the upper bridge are two open courts, one separating the garage and forming the entry, the other connecting the main house to the guesthouse and pool. A deck links these courts on the north and connects to paths that lead into the landscape with walks up the hill.

Exterior walls are clad in Corten steel plate; viewed from beyond, the rusty bar bridges the golden grass slopes. (Images 22, 23)

The interior is a continuous, white, light line. Service pods float in the bars of space. Full height sliding glass doors frame and open to the view and sound of the creek, which animates the house.

The entire roof is a photovoltaic field that converts California sunshine into energy. Major materials are renewable and recyclable.

A blue pool branches off the red bar and projects from the hill.

23

24

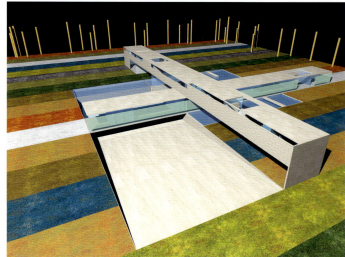
26

25

27

The Bar Houses emerged at the height of the Dot-com boom in the Bay Area. The technological revolution, powered by an intoxicating sense of changing the world, exploded and players were left with wealth of a type previously known only to corporate tycoons and movie stars.

Our clients were diversifying stock income into real estate by building huge homes or second residences in the country. The scale of optimism and extent of wealth allowed broad pleasures, and programs began to aspire to the level of Villas, Chateaux and Castles. Our problem was to provide forms for these desires, and I paged through Banister Fletcher often, trying to locate precedents and find their place in the chain of history.

There were multiple houses to work on simultaneously, one after and on top of the other, and at first it was just afterimage, but then it became conscious…a desire…the project. The results are the Bar Houses.

This work is in the legacy of type, rather than the prototype so prevalent in modern residential architecture. It is a shift from our earlier work where each house was conceived as an independent essay on a particular site and program, to an attitude about serialization, evolution, and refinement.

These houses display the effect of the technology itself; the power of visualization and exploration the computer facilitates. The use of this tool to create environments of precision. Its natural ability for duplication. The implication of the ethos of the electronic world's ephemeralization and reduction of matter and formality. The shift from building as machine to building as computer, the potential of these new technologies, with smart electronics, to dwell in worlds of heightened sensation and minimization, closer to nature.

The sites were mostly north of San Francisco, mostly in the beautiful rolling landscapes of Marin, Napa, and Sonoma. Typically, views abounded in all directions, sometimes with valleys or the distant Pacific, other times hills and foothills covered in native oaks, or open grasses edged with distant fog.

Bars of space lace their sites and act as barometers, measuring the topography without interrupting the terrain running through. Each is cartography, inscribing and describing its site.

Their abstract geologies do not impose but expose. They are sub monumental, forgetting the future rather than remembering the past, expanding the realm of space and diminishing the role of form.

28

29

30

These houses of constructed emptiness are more akin to mirrors than images, frames than pictures, more focused on time and event than object and monument.

The services are solid elements, which comb the space with walls of mechanism and storage floating within the lines.

They are buildings invented by threading and weaving, by making holes in things, or making things that make holes in things that are not, doubling the spaces of opportunity. The bars twist and fold, cross and loop, circle and lap, bridge and divide. At their intersections are sectional expansions and vertical connections.

The interest is in reflection, refraction, transparency, translucency and lightness, in ephemeral objects of absence and silence, in forms which fold on themselves, slipping and sliding through space as they frame and connect.

NOTES ON THE TRADITION OF TYPE
What follows is a map, plotting the route, showing the signposts that have pointed in the direction of these Bar Houses.

PALLADIO
In exhuming the body of work of Andrea Palladio, one discovers not only the first application of the Art of Architecture previously devoted to Church and State in the service of the Private Sector, but also the development of a type, a suite of houses based on theme and variation. A vocabulary of elements, box, wing, pediment, arcade, are disposed in varying combinations to accommodate to program and topography. This kit of parts is a return to classical forms, to the Architecture of Rome, assembled with traditional syntax and composition in overall form and detail.

FRENCH RENAISSANCE
The French Renaissance produced monuments of lavish expenditure on architecture and the decorative arts. These country palaces and castles were more picturesque than classical, more Gothic and romantic, more imbued with fantasy. The turreted apparition of Chateau Chamboard floats in a moat. Bars of rooms are strung along in enfilade, room after room, as the prototypical system of arrangement. Wings branch and turn to capture courts and gardens edged by moats and lakes. Landscape and water are designed with equal detail and intensity as rooms and galleries.

ENGLISH RENAISSANCE
The English Renaissance produced a collection of estate houses composed of arms stretching out into the countryside,

31

32

typically bars of rooms arranged enfilade, or along single loaded halls, with double loaded halls at the central masses. An alphabet of compositions are the legacy: U shaped Hatfield House, I shaped Bramshill, E shaped Aston Hall, B shaped Blickling Hall, H shaped Holland House, O shaped Hardwick Hall, etc.

JAPANESE SPACE

My first visit to Japan in June 1995 changed my perspective. It reinforced the realization I had experienced in the Barcelona Pavilion when I felt a mind shift from an interest in mass and enclosure to space and emptiness. I was awed by the translucent light of the shoji, the liquidity of space, the sense of repose, the presence of the sublime, the mystery of the veil, the enchantment of the boundless. I understood the idea of serenity as a silent guest in the home, the simplicity of refinement, the wealth of the austere, the simultaneous engagement of mind and sense, the reductive essential, the power of ceremony. This all may have to do with Shinto, the indigenous mixture of religious beliefs whose practice centers on the worship of kami or spirits through the sanctification of place rather than the presentation of image.

MIES

The plan of the brick country house of 1922 has been an underlay of thought so many times ... the walls shooting out into the landscape, the sense of the plinth, of garden spiraling into dense mass as program privatized. In June 1986 I visited the Barcelona Pavilion. There I realized what space is and experienced what a fish may when it first grasps that it lives in water. I suddenly understood the realm of radical architecture. Being inside made me float, and I took huge breaths, filling my lungs with air.

LE CORBUSIER

The Dom-ino house of 1914 provided Le Corbusier with a framework and was the key to almost all his houses up to 1935. This system was also the underpinning of his architectural production of other buildings of larger scale, the Unite, the Assembly Building at Chandigarh, the Mill Owners building, and his late Houses in India, including the Shodan House. Together with the five points of a new architecture, this system was the type for a complete oeuvre, a structure in which seemingly inexhaustible invention found its frame.

33

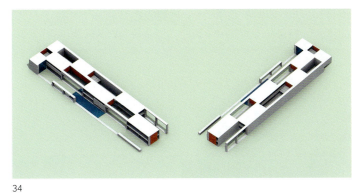
34

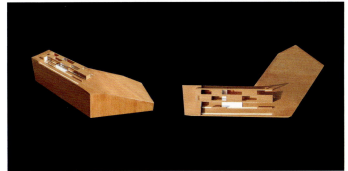
35

36

37

38

39

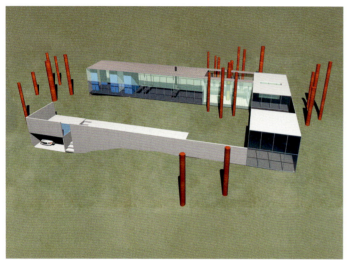
40

41

WEISSENHOFSEIDLUNG

This real time exhibition of "The Dwelling" orchestrated by Mies van der Rohe presented an entirely new stylistic expression with the same authority as building styles of the past. The modern dwelling, the "house as machine for living" was displayed fully realized, as a district, in many variants, as a complete vision of the new era. Still today, the socially radical neighborly relationships, the freedom of the interior planning, and the modest and powerful aesthetics are impressive.

THE USONIAN HOUSE

The array of Prarie Houses built by Wright in the first half of the Twentieth Century led to the dream of a broadly affordable and popular organic house for the masses of Broadacre City. Embracing the media, Wright propagated an array of affordable private houses for typical American families. Aimed at the average household, the hope was to provide quality design for popular housing.

As well as spatial innovations characteristic of the Wright oeuvre, there were significant technical advances….slab on grade, radiant heat, post and beam framing, board and batten cladding, etc.

CASE STUDY HOUSES

Conceived as low-cost experimental prototypes, John Entenza of *Arts and Architecture Magazine* supported the design of 36 case study houses from 1945 to 1966. The aim was to provide models for the buoyant post war building boom. These modern homes focussed on experimentation with simple industrial materials and construction and pronounced indoor outdoor relationships. They epitomized the optimism of the open and sublime freedom of the post war era. They built on a tradition of residential architecture already established by Gill, Wright, Schindler and Neutra. These houses became a laboratory of experimentation with materials, construction and aesthetics which epitomized the Californian Dream.

EICHLER

Inspired by Wright, and building on the Case Study House Program, the tract house developer Eichler found a way to mass produce affordable modern family homes in Northern California from the mid-50's to the mid-70's. Hiring three architectural firms to design prototypes, he developed a series of models which featured unashamed modernity and synthesized house and garden in the Japanese tradition. This provided a perfect

42

format for Northern Californian climate and life, and a serious challenge to the ubiquitous tracts of "Cape Cod" and "Ranch".

MINIMAL ART
Minimal art, emerging as a critique of abstract expressionism, aimed at maximum tension with minimal means. Expansion replaced abstraction in an expanded field of exclusions and absences. Elemental formal vehicles, free of reference, in repetition, serial, variation, intersection, establish relationships with situations and materials.

Minimal Art, especially through the work and writing of Robert Smithson, demonstrated a new paradigm of relationships with the natural. Much closer to the operations of nature than formal organic continuity, process rather than form was the object.

MINIMALISM
Extreme formal abstractions of the existing vocabulary of modernism became a formal project in the late 90's. This work is characterized by the process of reduction, by the concept of emptying, especially of meaning, and stringent and sophisticated use of materials, lucidity, translucency, and lightness. Through counterform, intense dialogue with the site is established. From Zen, the sense of repose, de-objectifying the built environment, and creating worlds of silence and reflection in response to the intensity of the end of the century, have become a goal.

LOFTS
Lofts have reinforced the lessons of the freeplan, of the generosity of volumetric space, of the proposition of indeterminate openness and fluidity. The lofty volume is as free from program as possible. Fixed service elements are compressed in service cores, floating in a sea of space, whose use is determined by furniture, slid around in the emptiness, allowing the domestic environment to become a liquid landscape, inhabited and changed by use. The loft is more like a frame than a picture, an instrument, an apparatus for living.

BAR HOUSES
The bar houses inhabit their sites without interruption. They are light as air. They are passage and flow, questioning the whole idea of interior they aim to barely exist. Considering their seeming similarity in plan, the variations in scale, materials and arrangements make these houses surprisingly different. (Images from 24 to 42)

APPENDIX

PROJECT CREDITS

Architect
Stanley Saitowitz /
Natoma Architects Inc.

Location
Atherton, California

Program
2 story and basement single family residence
with pool house, guest house and garages

Project Construction
January, 2017

Project Team
Stanley Saitowitz
Neil Kaye
Michael Luke
Steven Sanchez

General Contractor
David Warner
Redhorse Constructors, I;nc.

Project Construction Manager
David Warner
Redhorse Constructors, Inc.

Interiors
Stanley Saitowitz

Owner
Withheld

Civil Engineer
Pete Carlino
Lea & Braze Engineering Inc

Structural
Peter Yu
Yu Structural Engineers

Mechanical
Matt Reistetter
Monterey Energy Group

Concrete
Adorno Construction

Windows
Fleetwood Glazing

Millwork
Provided by owners of modular systems

Pool
Aquascape Pools

Hardware
Omnia

Garage Door
Custom fabricated

Electrical
Claussen Electric

Plumbing
Skaates Plumbing

Structural Steel
SR Freeman

Lighting
Anna Kondolf
Anna Kondolf Lighting Design

Audio Visual
Cliff Roepke
Site and Sounds

Rendering
Stanley Saitowitz

Model Construction
Stanley Saitowitz

Photography
Bruce Damonte
Richard Barnes

PHOTOGRAPHY CAPTIONS

The Master Suite floating over the Family Wing Terrace

The Master Suite Bridge framing the garden and floating over the Basement light Court

All glass side of the house shielded from the street

Living Room with floating glass encased fireplace, skylight and groundlight

Address introducing the design ideas

Master Suite hovering above the Basement

Two Ls intertwined and overlapping, building the site with walls and bridges framing courts and voids

Ls of Master Suite (left) and Living Room (right) capturing the view.

Two Ls balance on each other pointing to the view of the Bay and San Francisco

Entry Gate and void beyond framed by the Master Suite Bridge

The solid side of the house facing the street and protecting the interior

Solid Street Side with Garages and Children's Wing above (right) and Entry Canopy (left)

190 | APPENDIX

 L shaped Entry Portico leading to Front Door – Bay and San Francisco views beyond

 Entry Portico, pond reflecting Bay beyond, and bridge

 Entry Portico with L shaped Entry Bridge over pond reflecting Bay beyond

 Pond, L shaped Entry bridge and Entry Portico

 Intersection of formal rooms (left) and family rooms (right)

 Kitchen, Mudroom Pod, Family Room and Pool

 Outlook from Kitchen to Main Garden Court

 Looking in and out to Family Room Terrace

 Paths to Family Room and Pool

 Family Room TV wall floating in bar with office behind (left)

 Formal Living Room primary seating area with secondary seating behind

 Looking towards Kitchen from Mudroom pod

 Looking up and out of the Living Room, with glass pod containing Powder and Coat Rooms behind

 Living Room open to garden court (left) and protected from street (right)

 Looking out of Living Room with skylight and groundlight

 Glass roofed Dining Room with groundlight

191

 Living Room open to terrace and view

 Intersection of Children's Wing (left) and Master Suite (right)

 Under Master Suite Bridge

 Master Suite corner

 Ls overlaid, Living Dining Kitchen wing (left), and Master Suite above (right) with Basement Court below

 Garden view from Master Suite

 Basement Court below, Kitchen bar above

 Master Suite Bridge connecting bars and threading garden with family entry path (left)

 Family Entry from Garage to Mudroom, sheltered by bridge

 Tunnel link from Garage to Mudroom

 Garden woven by Ls and Bridges into courts

 Glass open face of house

 Solid Floating Master Suite protected from street

 The Kitchen from the pool edging the stair to the Basement level below

 Glass Floating Master Suite shielded from the street

 Main Garden Court shielded by house walls

 Living Room Terrace hovering over Basement

 Livingroom Overhang shading Basement Family Room Terrace

 Living Room projecting over Basement Terrace

 Floating Ls

 Floating Transparencies

 Family Room closed

 Family Room open

 Poolhouse/Guesthouse, pool and garden

 Family side of house with Pool

 Poolhouse/Guesthouse

 Hovering Transparencies

 Poolhouse/Guesthouse

 Evening

 Leaving

 Evening

DESIGNERS

Stanley Saitowitz was born in Johannesburg, South Africa, and received his Bachelor of Architecture at the University of Witwatersrand in 1974 and his Master's in Architecture at the University of California, Berkeley in 1977. He is Professor Emeritus of Architecture at the University of California, Berkeley. He has held several other prestigious academic positions, including the Elliot Noyes Professor at Harvard University GSD, the Bruce Goff Professor at University of Oklahoma, Norman, as well as teaching at UCLA, Rice, SCIARC, Cornell, Syracuse, the University of Texas at Austin and the University of the Witwatersrand, Johannesburg. He has given more than 250 public lectures in the United States and abroad. His first house was built in 1975, and together with Stanley Saitowitz|Natoma Architects Inc., has completed many buildings and projects. He has designed houses, housing, master plans, offices, museums, libraries, wineries, synagogues, churches, commercial and residential interiors, memorials, urban landscapes and promenades. Amongst many awards, the Transvaal House was declared a National Monument by the Monuments Council in South Africa in 1997, the New England Holocaust Memorial received the Henry Bacon Medal in 1998, and in 2006 he was a finalist for the Smithsonian Cooper Hewitt National Design Award given by Laura Bush at the White House. Four previous books have been published on the work, and articles have appeared in national and international magazines and newspapers. His paintings, drawings and models have been exhibited in numerous galleries and museums.

Neil Kaye is a Partner. He studied Environmental Science and Architecture at the University of Waterloo, Canada. He graduated on the Dean's Honor list and was awarded the AIA medal in his graduating year. Prior to joining Stanley Saitowitz|Natoma Architects in 1998, he worked with Bing Thom Architects and Busby Associates in Vancouver. During his 20 years with Natoma Architects, he has worked on projects both nationally and internationally, holding professional licenses in several US states and in Canada. Neil has developed a keen interest for complex mixed-use projects. He is currently working on several projects with over 2 million square feet of combined development. Recent projects include 8 Octavia; in-fill housing in San Francisco, The Palladium; a twin mixed use tower in Los Angeles, 1111 Sunset; a high rise in Los Angeles, and 188 Hooper; a new 500 bed student housing complex in San Francisco. As project architect he helped to lead the teams that successfully delivered The Tampa Museum of Art in Florida, Beth Sholom Synagogue in San Francisco and Uptown Mixed-use Development in Cleveland. He continues to play a key role in helping to develop the practice's nationally recognized strategies in delivering high quality lower cost housing units by leveraging efficiencies in building systems, pre-fabrication and innovative construction technologies.

Michael Luke, Project Architect, has been with Stanley Saitowitz|Natoma Architects for over twenty-five years. His broad-based experience is a byproduct of working on a wide range of building types, of varying scales and programs, with diverse owner and user groups. His work has taken him from Hawaii, to California, and currently throughout the country. As Project Architect he utilizes his design and technical experience to lead complex projects from schematic design through construction. Projects he has managed include Yerba Buena Lofts, Beth El Synagogue, New England Holocaust Memorial, UCSF Mission Bay Garage, and Uptown Cleveland. He received a Bachelor of Architecture from the University of Hawaii and a Master's of Architecture from the Southern California Institute of Architecture. As LEED AP, he oversees the sustainability goals of projects.

Team Members
Stanley Saitowitz, Michael Luke, Neil Kaye, Steve Snachez

BUILDERS

David Warner is the founder and owner of Redhorse Constructors (1981-present). For the past four decades he has been working on new urban formations around sustainable and resilient infrastructure and construction systems, serving as an advisor to startups that are creating new materials and systems for this new urban design intent. For instance, Redhorse has been selected to be the construction advisor for Ecoblock, an urban sustainability project whose partners include NASA and the California Energy Commission (CEC). This will be the first-of-its-kind block to demonstrate neighborhood-scale solutions to urban resilience, including energy and water efficiency, a communal solar-powered microgrid, and shared electric transportation. The project is led by UC Berkeley.

David is the co-founder of Human Needs Project (2010-present) with Connie Nielsen, a collaboration of academic and industry leaders who are in partnership with local communities to address the lack of basic services common in underserved urban populations. HNP's project in Kenya, the Kibera Town Center, provides basic services (water, toilets, showers, laundry) and empowerment services (business skills training, microcredit, WiFi, health kiosk, green marketplace) to over 800 people per day, demonstrating that clean, local energy can empower vibrant and sustainable community centers. HNP has deployed energy systems with the Rockefeller Foundation. With grant monies, HNP's market based poverty solution concept has been reviewed by Johns Hopkins University for scale up potential.

As a result of David's interest in new technologies, materials and concern for the environment, he has acted as technical advisor on a number of projects, including Sir David Adjaye's submittal for the Obama Presidential Center in Chicago and Sir Richard Branson's project for island development and sustainability focusing on low cement concrete recipes. In 2006, David co-founded Above Board Technologies, which built a pilot factory in Canada to prove that waste wheat could be used to compose a structurally rated panel to compete with plywood. In 2007 his efforts in sustainable construction and the implementation of green technologies in residential projects earned him the title Builder of the Year by the NAHB (USA region). David collaborated with Ojjo on a patent, which has installed municipal-grade foundation systems for the Gemini solar project, the largest in the U.S.

With a focus on green building, David has turned Redhorse into one of the nation's premier custom home builders, receiving a number of awards from the AIA, projects published in *Scientific American* and *Architectural Digest*, including achievement awards from local and industry organizations. David's career has ranged from building sophisticated architectural structures, high performance recording studios, Island energy infrastructure, and biodynamic ranches. Having worked in all these arenas, he brings the combination of technology, infrastructure, construction and art into a unified process where material selection and system performance are blended. In 2023, David was awarded a patent for his Plank System, a non-concrete foundation which has established a new form of exoskeleton for the future of housing that has less embodied energy, fast deployment and is resilient to climate impacts due to its engineering properties and low-cost design. David was able to showcase the Plank System concept at a ribbon-cutting event at the University of California, Davis in May 2024 with California leaders in building, tech, academia and policy making in attendance.

David received his undergraduate degree from the College of Natural Resources at the University of California, Berkeley in 1976 and his teaching credential in Biology from San Francisco State in 1977. He has been an advisory board member at UC Berkeley College of Natural Resources Advisory since 2015.

Redhorse is not just a building company. As innovators in sustainability and construction technology, we live by the mantra "there is no stop." When others say it can't be done, we use our imagination, resolve and wealth of skilled talent to find a way and move forward. We are committed to running projects smoothly, efficiently, and cost effectively, no matter the complexity. With over 40 years of expertise, we thrive on providing practical solutions to all areas of construction, such as difficult site conditions, integration of green building technologies, sophisticated mechanical and energy systems, and time/budget constraints. We attribute our success in the industry to open communication, proactive construction management, mentorship of co-workers and efficiency on our job sites. As Redhorse has grown and matured into an exceptional special services builder, we have formed great relationships with many of the leading design professionals, sub-contractors and material fabricators in the Bay Area and beyond.